Adding Layers

Color, Design & Imagination

15 ORIGINAL QUILT PROJECTS

from Kathy Doughty of Material Obsession

stashBOOKS.

an imprint of C&T Publishing

Text copyright © 2014 by Kathy Doughty

Photography and Artwork copyright © 2014 by C&T Publishing, Inc.

Publisher: Amy Marson

Creative Director: Gailen Runge

Art Director: Kristy Zacharias

Editor: S. Michele Fry

Technical Editors: Alison M. Schmidt and Daniel Rouse

Cover/Book Designer: April Mostek

Production Coordinators: Zinnia Heinzmann and Karen Ide

Production Editor: Alice Mace Nakanishi

Illustrator: Jenny Davis

Photo Assistant: Mary Peyton Peppo

Style and Flat Photography by John Doughty, unless otherwise noted; How-To Photography by Diane Pedersen and Nissa Brehmer of C&T Publishing, Inc., unless otherwise noted

Published by Stash Books, an imprint of C&T Publishing, Inc., P.O. Box 1456, Lafayette, CA 94549

Library of Congress Cataloging-in-Publication Data

Doughty, Kathy.

 Adding layers : color, design & imagination : 15 original quilt projects from Kathy Doughty of Material obsession.

    pages cm

 ISBN 978-1-60705-847-2 (soft cover)

1. Patchwork--Patterns. 2. Quilting--Patterns. I. Title.

 TT835.D693 2014

 746.46--dc23

                              2013024143

Printed in China

10 9 8 7 6 5 4 3 2 1

Contents

PROJECTS

Dedication

I am nothing without my husband, John, and my three sons, Oscar, Noah, and Sam. Outside the family are my MO quilting sisters—Bundle Caldwell, Cath Babidge, Wendy Williams, Carolyn Davis, Gai Collins, Grace Widders, Kate Page, Megan Manwaring, Liesel Moult, and Robyn Shipton. These women make the shop my happy place to work and visit. And thank you to the wonderful team at C&T that has made me look so much better than I am!

Introduction

Making Connections

Quiltmakers are the storytellers of each generation. The quilts we make leave a legacy of time and place in a manner that appeals to many senses and captures moments in time. The lives and voices of the makers are sewn into a composite piece of visual delight that evocatively joins color, technique, and style into a long-lasting memory. We see and can imagine a quilt wrapped warmly around a newly married couple, protecting a baby against the elements, flapping in the breeze on the clothesline, or lying folded in an attic for decades. We see the stories of lives and events woven with a long piece of thread. We need to be a part of what we see, and so we make quilts to connect. We make our own stories that reflect where we are now, what we see, and what we have to say about our lives. Contemporary quilters layer textiles, technique, and imagination to make a reflection of the present world for those who follow.

Seeing a quilt immediately leads us to ask a series of questions. Who made the quilt? Where was it made? What was the motivation that ultimately ended up as this quilt? We look for clues in the fabric, the technique, and the style to tell us more about the maker. What attracts our attention may be obvious or subtle. We may see all the delights of a given quilt at once, or we may go on a long walk of discovery that delights us in numerous small revelations. We can easily fall in love with a quilt and want it to be ours! We become aware of what we like or don't like as we view a quilt with admiration or aversion. Walk through any quilt show, and you will hear the participants expressing their varied opinions about how a quilt makes them react, much like viewers examining a treasured piece of art.

What strikes me is how a simple quilt can move the mind and heart. Quilts in their essence are layers of color, pattern, and imagination, all working together to form a composite textile product. Fashion and function are decoratively fused. The top layer tells the obvious story about decisions regarding color and pattern and relates in spirit to the fashion of the day. The middle layer adds warmth, texture, and dimension as it works unseen from within. The backing holds it all together. Each layer has a role to play. We travel with the makers of the past and present into the future in our mind's eye, learning, feeling, experiencing, and imagining what was, is, and will be while leaving a telling treasure for those who follow.

MY JOURNEY

Quilters all start somewhere. Some of us were guided into a life of sewing at an early age by our mothers or grandmothers. The memory of the care and love they expressed is closely associated with the process. Others discovered sewing at school, or even later in life. I am one of those late-blooming quilters. Although I had many opportunities to pick up a needle when I was young, it wasn't until I was making a home of my own that the idea really stuck. At first I was attracted to the process of using scraps of fabric to make a textile treasure. One thing led to another as I discovered more about how to use process and technique to develop pattern with color, line, and shape. More than twenty years later, I can see that quilting has brought much joy to my life, and I have much to be grateful for as a result. What amazes me is that no matter how far I dig into the process, I always find more—more color combinations, more patterns to try, more techniques to learn, and more, more, more fun!

The plot of my quilting story thickens. Of all the elements of the quilt, the one I love the most is the story that I hear in my head as I make it. The issues of the day, the weather, music, and even TV often become part of the memories that make up the story of each quilt. In sewing the elements together, I am creating a lasting impression of where I am today, right now, for everyone to see. Just as important as the *how* of making the quilt is the *why*. My imagination works overtime sewing the story of each quilt.

When my shop, Material Obsession, was new ten years ago, we were pushing existing boundaries while working unexplored new territories in layout, fabrics, and design for quilts. First, we wanted easy. Then quick. Quick and easy results fit into a busy life. In a world filled with chicks and country colors, we were using color-fully printed fabrics with large graphics, spots, and stripes. Eyes would widen upon entering the shop. Whispers of "This shop will never last!" were heard many times, along with grumbles that our methods "aren't quilting." A strong determination won out, and now the new techniques are widely accepted as a sign of our times.

You and the Book

I am a self-taught quilter. Over the years I have accumulated many skills that have added interest and depth to my quilting experience, both literally and figuratively. Like a child, I walked before I ran. Simple fabric selections, basic patterns, and obvious designs gave way to more mature, thoughtful, and developed creations. Quilting is one area in my life that allowed me to go slowly, revealing in layers a growing depth of understanding. The square gave way to triangles, wedges, and appliqué. Simple palettes grew more complex. My story started changing to include subplots. The following chapters explore areas of quilting that are important to me—stories that have grown from simple concepts to include new fabric choices, new techniques, and a lot of imagination.

Every quilter is different and has personal reasons for making quilts. It may be an attraction to the fabric, the geometry, the history, the process, or the result, but in any case patchwork quilting has an endless supply of options. This book provides a path to developing layers of depth and understanding in your process. Chapter 1 (page 20) deals with working with fabrics. It is helpful to work within your collection of fabrics, your stash. We buy fabrics because we love them, and now it is time to use them! In Chapter 2 (page 58) we travel beyond the simple straight cut and use a few tools to enhance our level of technical expertise. Tools are a great way to extend our skill base accurately. Chapter 3 (page 92) introduces a bit of imagination. What happens if we change an element of a quilt? In this case, we examine scale.

As you progress through the book, I challenge you to find methods for expanding your basic ideas and habits. At the start of each quilt project, ask yourself, "What do I want to say?" Like the stitches that bind one layer to the others, the layering of fabric, design, and a bit of imagination creates unique opportunities within each step of the creative process. At the end, your quilt will be your own, representing your life, thoughts, feelings, and experiences. Depending on your choices, you can make a pop-song quilt— one that has immediate impact with modern lines and popular, fashionable fabrics—or you can arrange a symphony of color and pattern in more traditional ways.

Tools of the Trade

Creativity

When designing a quilt I usually have a concept in mind based on an image, a photo, or a tool that I want to use. I turn on the music and let the left (or is it right?) side of my brain relax. Then I let the flow of creativity take over. At this stage it is important to listen to and then trust your instincts. If it feels right, go forward; if it doesn't, grab a cup of coffee and your camera and have a bit of a think. Doubt is part of the process! Try to stay focused on the quilt at hand and make consistent decisions in regard to the original design concept. It might become necessary to change things along the way, but that is all part of the process.

Stash Fabric

Remember when you walked into a shop and found a fabric you absolutely had to have? You bought it, took it home—and now it haunts you from the shelf where it is stored. Collecting fabric has become a popular pastime. It is nice to fold it, stack it, sort it, and imagine all the wonders it could become. Having said that, the best thing to do with your stash is to use it! After many years, I actually took the time to organize my stash into color groups. I can see at a glance where I might start looking for a fabric. I know what I have and, just as important, what I don't have.

COLOR—warm or cool

MONOCHROMATIC OR POLYCHROMATIC—single or multiple colors

VALUE—light or dark

GRAPHIC INTEGRITY—spot, stripe, or solid background piece

INSPIRATION FABRIC—the one that holds the quilt together

FUSSY CUTTING—feature images or a fantastic graphic repeat

QUANTITY—a lot of a fabric or just a treasured scrap

FASHION—a modern or vintage fabric

DIRECTION—a directional pattern

Antique quilts have wonderful appeal created by a sense of make-do and a random use of fabric. We can imagine that the leftover fabrics from a dress didn't fully fit the requirements of a border, or a similar substitution was used to finish a pattern repeat. These choices made out of necessity offer intrigue and interest as we wonder what happened to what we expected to see. We can achieve a sense of this resourcefulness by using our stash. Make decisions based on what is available and create a sense of individual choice. If the perfect fabric isn't available, find another one that works. Not only can this be a fun challenge but the slight variation of pattern created adds a great deal of interest.

Spend time absorbing the look of the fabric and understanding how it can be used. Consider if you need a feature fabric, a graphic or directional print, or a spacer. Let the fabrics dictate where they should be used. That is the first step in making quilts that tell your story.

Remember that we are creatures of habit. We get into routines in our lives and find security in making decisions that we know and understand. Making unique quilts requires courage and a willingness to experiment. Be prepared to change direction, add something different, or take something away. Feel the fabric, move it around your stash, look at it in different light, and audition a variety of options. What you are looking for is the "Aha!" moment—the moment when two fabrics excite each other. Wait for it; it will happen!

Design Wall

As a designer, I view my design wall as my best friend. I use the wall to audition combinations of shapes, color choices, and scale. To start, I cut a variety of fabrics, place them on the wall, and move them around. At this stage I often pull out my camera. The camera reveals the overall balance of the project by diminishing the detail. I often see patterns evolving that may not have been obvious at the start. By using the design wall I also can experiment with little to no commitment to the design until I am sure. Like any form of exercise, working an idea gives us strength; we then use the design wall to make choices and decide where we want to end up.

Concepts

In days gone by, American women would sit and mostly stitch by hand with little light. The result was a world of small fiddly blocks that fit in the lap. The women shared their blocks with each other to create trends that moved from Baltimore to the Wild West. One day I decided that although originally small, traditional blocks could be made *big*, and it would be fresh and interesting. What would happen if I simply enlarged the traditional 6″ block to 60″? Wow! I loved the result. The large blocks work beautifully with my contemporary fabrics. To maintain the link to the traditional, I like to include an aspect of tradition somewhere in the quilt. In some cases it might be the fabric, where in others it might be piecing the background with small shapes.

Once the barrier of traditional restraint gives way, a beautiful mix of old and new starts to appear.

Quilting

Deciding how to quilt is an important decision for every quilt. The popularity of machine quilting, both domestic and professional, has grown in recent years, with good reason. However, hand quilting is a joyful process. When I am quilting, my hands are busy, my brain relaxes, and the process is soothing. So much of my life happens in quick time that the opportunity to slow down and enjoy the handwork of yesteryear is something I eagerly add to my to-do list. Having a quilt to pick up while on the go and mindlessly progressing through the rows of stitching is a practice that offers great reward at the end of a hectic day. Slowly but surely the work comes together and is eventually ready to be bound!

The idea of sewing eleven stitches to the inch has never appealed to me, but using perle cotton size 8 and big stitches does. The technique is easy to master in a short practice session. This method also allows me to add texture and color to the quilt. I use three to five colors in most quilts. In some cases I might use only one color, but it is fun to have a bowl of colorful perle cottons at my side and to choose colors that enhance the blocks being quilted. Everyone's stitches will be different, so quantities may vary. When you are using only one color, I recommend two balls for twin-size quilts and three to five balls for larger quilts.

The tools for quilting are easy to find and are outlined in the equipment section following, but suffice it to say that large needles (embroidery needles size 3–9), a solid hoop, a chalk pencil, and a collection of perle cottons will put you well on your way to finishing your quilt in your own style.

Tools

Visual appeal in a quilt is achieved by the right mix of fabrics, a balanced design, and a bit of imagination. However, it is also important that the quilt lies flat, that seams join, that the lines of the design are distinguished, and that in the end the quilt is square—not to mention sewn together in a manner that will stand the test of time and wear. To achieve accurate results I employ three tools: graph paper, the design wall, and acrylic rulers/templates. When using these items I can experiment and cut accurately, confident that my quilt will assemble properly and then lie flat.

So, how do we get there? I find using acrylic templates accompanied by my handy rotary cutter and mat invaluable.

Rotary cutters are readily available. Different people like different handles, so choose one that is comfortable for you. The blades are easily replaced when blunt, but the handle should last a lifetime if handled properly (and maybe labeled for quilt groups or classes!). Small blades are handy for cutting out circles and templates.

RULERS AND TEMPLATES

I recommend these, in this order!

HALF-SQUARE TRIANGLE RULERS You'll want a good half-square triangle ruler with the points cut off to reveal a flat-tip point. They vary in size, but an 8½″ ruler is a standard size for multiple project use. Some people like a 4½″ or 12½″ as well. The blunt point allows for figuring sizes based on ½″ plus the finished size of the square. This simple adjustment makes cutting strips and then sewing them together much easier. Large half-square triangle rulers are good for side setting blocks.

60° RULERS/TEMPLATES Good-sized 60° rulers allow for accurate cutting of equilateral triangles, diamonds, half-diamonds, and half-triangles. A must for moving beyond the square.

SQUARE Squares are sometimes expensive in the larger sizes, but they can prove invaluable. They come in a variety of sizes, from 4½″ to 20½″. The largest are helpful for squaring up pieced blocks or appliqué shapes, trimming blocks, trimming quilts for binding, and general shaping of projects.

WEDGE RULERS Wedges come in a variety of sizes, but they all end up making a circle, which is 360°. Wedges look tricky but are in fact simple to use. They come in a variety of degrees. To make a circle block, remember the following:

- 10° wedge ruler needs 36 wedges
- 15° wedge ruler needs 24 wedges
- 18° wedge ruler needs 20 wedges
- 22½° wedge ruler needs 16 wedges

Easy. Cutting the same measured segments on the wedge creates a circle. Wedges can be joined along the long sides to form circles. The tips can be folded in and sewn for Dresden Plates, or the circle can be trimmed to be square. It is also possible to flip the narrow and short ends of the wedges and join them to form borders or frames. Experiment and have some fun!

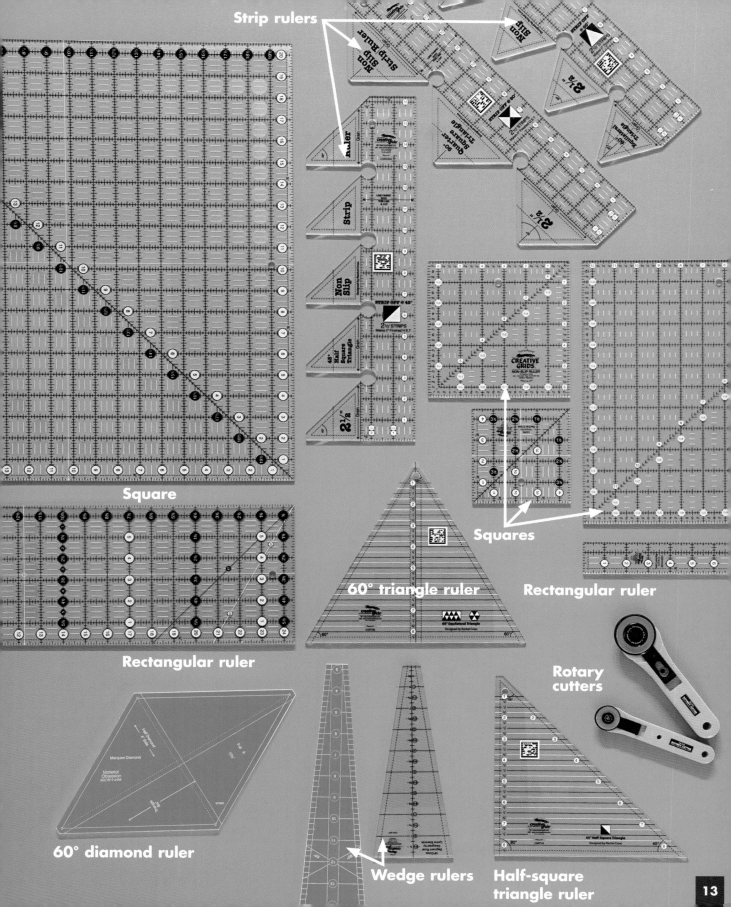

Strip rulers

Square

Rectangular ruler

60° diamond ruler

60° triangle ruler

Squares

Rectangular ruler

Rotary cutters

Wedge rulers

Half-square triangle ruler

Cutting Strips

My preferred method of cutting strips is one I learned from Marti Michell. It ensures accuracy by keeping the fabric in position throughout the cutting process. Try this method, which at first might seem awkward but will soon become natural.

To start, establish a straight edge. Fold the fabric with selvages together and, with the fold nearest you, trim the right-hand raw edge to be straight (**A**).

Position the measuring ruler along the trimmed edge, covering the strip width you wish to cut, and bring in a second long ruler to the inside edge (to the left of the measuring ruler) (**B**).

Now move the measuring ruler away and cut against the right-hand edge of the second ruler to make a strip (**C**).

Continue to measure with the first ruler and cut with the second ruler until you have enough strips. This method works for all types of rectangular rulers (**D**).

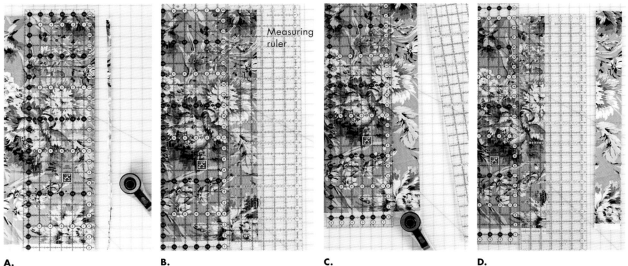

A.   B.   C.   D.

Cutting Wedges from Strips

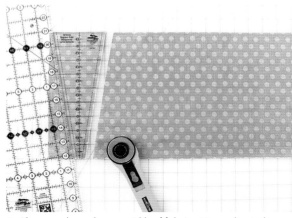

A. Place wedge ruler on width-of-fabric strip and cut along right side of wedge.

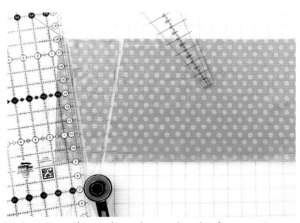

B. Remove wedge and cut along right side of rectangular ruler to yield first wedge.

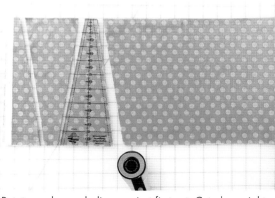

C. Rotate wedge and align against first cut. Cut along right side to yield second wedge.

D. Continue across strip, alternating wedge placement from top to bottom.

These are the template shapes that I recommend for basic quiltmaking. From there it is easy to start collecting shapes that are more specific to the blocks you want to make. For example, in the quilt *Follow the Sun* (page 42) I used premade acrylic templates from a Queen of the May block design. The acrylic shapes allow for the pieces of the block to be cut out accurately and have joining points indicated for ease in marking and sewing. The fun part is that they allow us to make more interesting blocks without using template plastic, which can alter during use and not be as accurate.

A variety of shapes are available on the market. Next time you are in a quilt shop take the time to review what is offered. At first the templates may look like foreign objects, but soon their value will become clear. Tools that inspire you to make quilts add value to your stash. It is easy to start making up quilts with the fabrics you own when you're inspired by a specific shape, block pattern, or design.

Using Special Rulers

The Creative Grids strip rulers come in 45°-, 60°-, and 90°-triangle variations, with new versions being added all the time. They are quickly becoming the handiest tools that I have in my studio for making interesting sashing, blocks, and borders.

Half-Square Triangle Units

Align two strips of fabric with right sides together. Position a 45° Strip Ruler for Half-Square Triangles with the blunt tips of the triangles at the top of the strip and use the rotary cutter to cut through both layers along the diagonal and vertical edges.

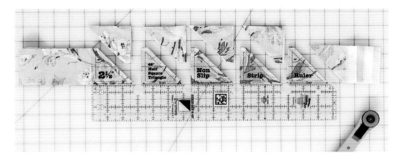

Pick up a pair of triangles, one from each strip, aligned as they were cut. With both blunt tips toward the sewing machine needle and right sides together, sew with a ¼″ seam allowance along the bias edge. Feeding the blunt tips of the triangles into the sewing machine first allows for easy engagement with the needle.

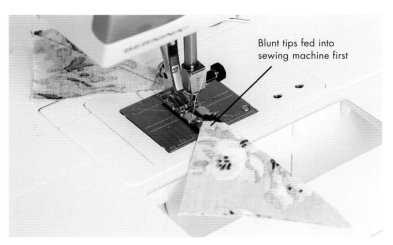

Blunt tips fed into sewing machine first

Quarter-Square Triangle Units

Repeat the strip cutting process as for the 45° strip ruler, but use the 90° strip ruler to cut quarter-square triangles (triangles with the bias on the two short sides).

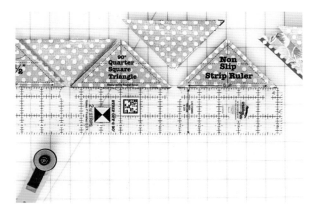

Four quarter-square triangles sewn into square block

Sashing strips can be made like this; they look great between blocks.

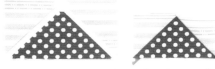

Working 45° and 90° strip rulers will make units for Flying Geese.

60° (Equilateral) Triangles

Repeat the strip cutting process with two fabric strips, right sides together, and use the 60° strip ruler in the same manner to cut pairs of equilateral triangles. The trick to using 60° triangles is remembering that one side of the triangle is on the straight grain of the fabric and two sides are on the bias and may stretch. After the triangles are cut, the straight grain side of each triangle will be opposite the blunt tip of the triangle. Keep the pairs of triangles together as they were cut for ease in sewing them together.

Sew the triangle pairs together along the bias edges with a ¼″ seam allowance, being careful not to stretch the edges as you sew. Be sure to always position the blunt tips of the triangles toward the sewing machine needle. The straight grain should remain on the outside edge of the pieced unit to avoid creating stretchy, hard-to-manage outer edges.

Bias edges

Straight-grain edge

Position triangles in row to make pieced strips.

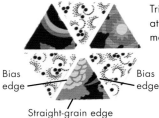

Triangles positioned with attention to value or color make hexagon patterns.

Bias edge

Bias edge

Straight-grain edge

OTHER TOOLS

NEEDLES

Appliqué: Milliners needles size 9 or 10 are fine and easy to manipulate when sewing needle-turn appliqué. I like a long needle, but it is up to you to determine what size needle feels comfortable and works for you.

Quilting: I have a large collection of embroidery needles sizes 3–9 because I almost always quilt with perle cotton size 8 or 12. The holes are a bit bigger for threading, and the shaft is also big enough to make a nice hole in the fabric for pulling through the slightly larger thread.

PERLE COTTONS SIZE 8 OR SIZE 12

I have a huge stash of colors of perle cottons, mainly size 8 but also size 12, so that when I get my quilt top done I can sit down and immediately get started quilting. I usually use three to five colors in my quilts, so having a wide range is a delight. I love having what I need when I want it!

CHALK PENCIL

I use chalk pencils to make quilting lines. When a straight line is required, I use a straightedge or masking tape with the chalk pencil to mark the line. When I want to make up the quilting lines in a more organic manner, I freehand draw the designs on with the chalk pencil and then follow the line with quilting. The benefit of chalk is that it always rubs off, and it comes in a variety of colors so it will show up no matter what color the fabric is.

QUILTING HOOP

A good-quality quilting hoop is an investment that when handled properly will last a lifetime. My hoop is a loved symbol of peace and quiet in my life! It holds the layers of my quilt together gently but securely. There are a variety of sizes, and it is important to choose one that is right for your body size. I have a 14″ that I use most of the time, but I also have a 16″ that I use when I am doing big designs or if I want to see the entire block while quilting.

APPLIQUÉ GLUE

Gluestick or glue pen: It is good to have a glue pen for semipermanent placement of fabrics in appliqué designs. Cutting out the shapes and temporarily placing them on the quilt allows for easy assessment of the design before everything is pinned, basted, or even sewn into place.

Bottled glue: This is great for dotting down a line for stems or fine lines for thicker fabrics. Be careful with the dotting glue, as too much can leave messy marks on the finished appliqué if it comes through the fabric.

SCISSORS

We all generally have a good pair of scissors. It is important to have a nice sharp pair of handled scissors exclusively for cutting fabric. It is also important to have a small pair with a sharp point to get into the curves of appliqué or for cutting thread ends. I also have a pair of curve-tipped scissors that are always by my side when I'm quilting or doing appliqué, as they help keep me from cutting into the fabric.

THREAD

There are a lot of threads on the market. Talk to the employees at your local quilt shop about what they carry and why. Choose a thread that is strong and high quality regardless of the cost, because one thing is for sure: you don't want it breaking in your machine or in your finished quilt if it can't handle the duty. For machine piecing 40-weight is fine, and for hand sewing I recommend a 50-weight. Over the years I have migrated to using Aurifil. It has a nice variety of colors and weights and is a high-quality product.

BATTING Batting is a subject that doesn't get enough coverage. Here are some simple guidelines I use when selecting batting for my quilts:

For hand quilting: My choice is nonscrim low-loft wool. I like the feeling of my needle gliding through the soft inner layer of the wool. It has a bit of texture when quilted, which I take into consideration. If the quilt has a lot of color variety, I prefer the lower-loft texture from quilting.

For machine quilting: My choice is usually low-loft wool for warmth or cotton for summer.

For antique or crib quilts: My choice for lightweight crib quilts or quilts that I want to look old is flannel.

Adding Layers—Color, Design & Imagination

CHAPTER 1
Working the Stash

Ah, the stash. We start it, build it, sort it, stack it, pack it, love it! Full of collected treasures, it defines us as quilters and becomes the topic of many conversations. The thrill of the hunt for the perfect fabrics reveals all types of personalities. There are those of us who buy a little and those who buy a lot. The simple act of collecting is a favorite pastime for many of us. As a shop owner I have heard many stories about stashes. I am often left with a curious feeling: Why collect fabric if it is never to be used? Especially because there is something special about a quilt made with what we have collected.

Selecting fabrics for a quilt should be a process filled with more delight than angst. Yes, it can be a challenge to pick fabrics, but one that should be filled with *fun*. Like many learning exercises, it's something we get better at as we go along. Choosing the fabric is about finding a common link. Once you have established that link, the rest is easy. It might be a theme like vintage fabrics; an inspiration fabric; or a design, a color range, or an image in the fabric—but whatever it is, stay focused as you select your fabrics. If a stash doesn't get used, it can appear dated. It is possible to activate the stash by adding one or two current fabrics. The new life adds interest, and you'll be surprised at how many fabrics you have that you can use!

Since discovering the Gee's Bend quilters and their view that chance is a great creative director, I have made that my motto but modified it slightly. I think chance is a great element, but thoughtful consideration makes the fabrics work harmoniously. That's what a stash quilt does best; it mixes up fabrics that may or may not be meant to go together—spots, florals, and all kinds of other fabrics somehow end up together as one thing, bringing home the element of chance.

Planning in advance can help you manage your stash. Organize your scraps as you make quilts. I have huge buckets of scraps from making quilts. As a whole they are unmanageable, but if I sort them by color groups, sizes, or shapes, they become more useful. The organizing is the key to using them up. Try trimming scraps to be squares, strips, or triangles as you make your quilts; then store like with like. They'll look much more appealing that way.

You selected it for whatever the reason.... Let's put it to good use!

Vintage Spin

30 FINISHED BLOCKS: 13″ × 13″ • **FINISHED QUILT:** 65″ × 78″ (165cm × 198cm)

How I Started

Over the years I have enjoyed collecting vintage fabrics. Some are a bit worn, some wrapped in plastic, some thrift shop clothes. I collect them because I love the designs. *Vintage Spin* is a quilt made from these specially collected fabrics that were old or just looked old. Where to start?

Make a pile of your "old"-looking fabrics. The fabrics are just part of the look—the trick to making quilts that look old is to try *not* to match! There are subtle links in all the pairs used in each block, but they don't necessarily look like they came from the same fabric line. This quilt is also a lesson in value. Although all the blocks have a light and a dark, not all of them have the same value variation. The eye moves from one light spot to another around the quilt, searching for discoveries.

MATERIALS

Yardage based on 42″ (107cm) usable WOF.*

FABRICS:

- 1 yard (1m) black for center circles and binding
- ⅓ yard (30cm) each of 30 light fabrics
- ⅓ yard (30cm) each of 30 dark fabrics

BACKING: 5 yards (4.6m)

BATTING: 73″ × 86″ (185cm × 220cm)

OPTIONAL TOOL: 18° wedge ruler, at least 9″ long

* WOF = width of fabric

CUTTING

Light and dark fabrics:

- Cut 1 strip 9″ × WOF from each light and dark fabric. Refer to Cutting Wedges from Strips (page 15) to subcut each strip into 10 wedges using the entire length of the wedge pattern provided (pullout page P1).

- Group the cut wedges into 30 sets of 10 pairs of matching light and dark wedges.

Black fabric:

- Using the pattern provided (pullout page P1), or a 3″ circular template, trace 30 circle shapes with chalk on the right side of the black fabric. Cut ¼″ outside the chalk line (or your preferred needle-turn appliqué seam allowance) to make 30 circle shapes. Finger-press the edges along the chalk line to the wrong side to make the appliqué easier.

Binding:

- Cut 8 strips 2½″ × WOF.

Second cut
Wedge template, 1st position
First cut
24″ ruler
Third cut
Wedge template, 2nd position

Assembly

All seam allowances are ¼″ unless otherwise noted.

1. Join a light and a dark wedge together along an angled edge as shown. Repeat to make 10 pairs.

Two wedges sewn along the length make a pair.

tip

Be sure to keep the same fabric on top when sewing so the pair fabrics alternate when sewn together.

2. Join the pairs and continue joining until the wedges make a circle. Turn over and gently press all the seam allowances to the dark side.

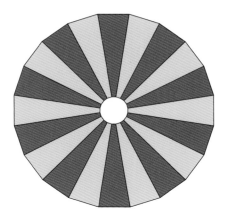

3. Using a large square ruler, trim the circle into a 13½″ × 13½″ square.

A. Position the square ruler so that the vertical center of the square will run through the middle of 2 dark wedges.

B. Check that the horizontal center of the square runs through 2 light wedges.

tip

Mark the ruler or template with masking tape to ensure that each circle is the same.

C. Ensure that the center of the circle is positioned in the center of the square. Trim around the edges to make the circle a 13½″ × 13½″ square.

4. Repeat Step 3 to make 30 blocks.

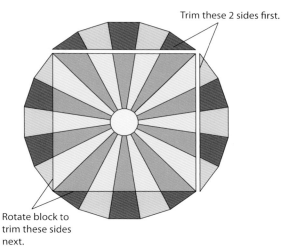

Trim these 2 sides first.

Rotate block to trim these sides next.

Trim to square up along the right side and across the top. Flip the block so that the square edges line up with the masking tape and trim again to make the square.

5. Position the cut circles in the center of each block and pin in place.

6. Appliqué the small circles to the middle of the squares.

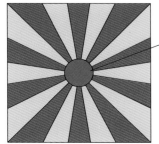

Appliqué circle over hole.

7. Repeat Steps 5 and 6 on all the blocks.

8. Lay out the squares in 6 rows of 5 blocks. Join the blocks together into rows. Match up and pin at the seam allowances to ensure that the wedges meet up. Note that the blocks connect with the light wedges moving horizontally, and dark wedges connect vertically where they meet.

9. Join the rows to complete the top.

10. Layer, baste, and quilt. Join the 8 binding strips end to end with diagonal seams and use to bind the quilt.

Quilt assembly diagram

How I Finished

I used a wool/cotton blend batting. It had scrim, which made it a tiny bit more resistant to hand quilting with perle cotton size 8. When I want a quilt to have vintage appeal, I use a low-loft batting. Another option would have been to use a flannel sheet to really make it look and feel authentic.

I quilted with black perle cotton size 12. The size 12 is slightly lighter weight than the 8, so, again, it lends to the antique look of the quilt. The quilting lines move through the circles on the flatter, or down, side of the seams. Pressing the seam allowances to the dark side when constructing the blocks means that the lines will usually move down the lighter fabric on the side where the seam allowances have been pressed away. Straight quilting lines don't take long and are good practice for getting the stitch size right.

House Party

How I Started

House Party started as a design from a 1930s pink quilt. As is often the case, I stared at it until I could see how I could make it. Kaffe Fassett's Field of Flowers was the inspiration fabric, which has a lot of bright colors that seemed to make my stash dance in pairs to a musical beat. Each pair works an element of contrast in varying degrees—some lights and darks, some warms and cools, some flowers and stripes. The fabrics include everything in my stash, from reproductions to Japanese.

The Folk Art fabric by Kaffe Fassett in the border was full of simple items from the home, which became the border appliqué that makes the house rock.

In the past there were certain blocks I would always avoid. They included anything with curves, appliqué, inset seams, or mitered seams. The more quilts I make, the more I am tempted to try new skills, and in trying I have mastered them. This quilt has inset seams throughout. If you want to avoid them, the quilt can come together easily with a few minor changes. I have included two different construction techniques. The first has inset seams and will produce the quilt in the photo. The second allows for a simpler method with straight seams for the quilt top assembly.

note
Read through the directions first and decide which method you would like to use to assemble the quilt.

MATERIALS

Yardage based on 42″ (107cm) usable WOF.*

note
When making stash quilts we sometimes find bits of fabric that are odd shapes. This quilt is easily made from scraps, so keep in mind that you only need 6 squares 2½″ × 2½″ from one fabric and 4 squares 2½″ × 2½″ *plus* a 4⅛″ × 4⅛″ square from a second fabric.

QUILT TOP:
- 128 different fabric scraps, each at least 4⅛″ × 15″, grouped into coordinating pairs for pieced units
- 2⅝ yards (2.4m) for borders
- 1¼ yards (1m) inspiration fabric for center squares and setting triangles
- 20 fat quarters or large scraps for border appliqué

BACKING: 8 yards (7.6m)

BINDING: ¾ yard (70cm)

BATTING: 92″ × 92″ (235cm × 235cm)

FREEZER PAPER: for appliqué

* *WOF = width of fabric*

Pieced Units

All seam allowances are ¼″ unless otherwise noted.

The pieced block assembly is the same for either method of construction.

1. From a scrap at least 4⅛″ × 15″, cut a strip 4⅛″ × the length of the scrap and subcut a square 4⅛″ × 4⅛″. Subcut it on the diagonal twice to make 4 quarter-square triangles (triangle A).

2. From the remaining scrap strip, cut 4 squares 2½″ × 2½″ (square A).

3. From a coordinating scrap, cut a strip 2½″ × the length of the scrap and subcut 6 squares 2½″ × 2½″ (square B).

4. Following the diagram, sew the A and B pieces together in rows and then join the rows.

Sew A and B pieces together into rows.

Sew rows together to make unit.

5. Repeat Steps 1–4 to make a total of 64 pieced units.

> **note**
>
> Put your sewn units on the design wall. Be prepared to make changes, additions, and assessments along the way. As the work progresses, it will start to tell you if it needs more warm fabrics or cool fabrics, or more lights or darks. Take a photo or look through a camera lens at the 64 total units to be sure that they are balanced throughout the quilt.

Assembly

When all the pieced units are made, select one of the two assembly options that follow.

ASSEMBLY OPTION 1 — *This will make the quilt as photographed.*

CUTTING

From inspiration fabric:

- Cut 5 strips 6⅛″ × WOF. Subcut 25 squares (C) 6⅛″ × 6⅛″.

- Cut 1 strip 9¼″ × WOF. Subcut 3 squares 9¼″ × 9¼″; subcut each square on the diagonal twice to make 12 quarter-square triangles (D).

- From the remaining fabric, cut 2 squares 4⅞″ × 4⅞″; subcut each square on the diagonal once to make 4 half-square triangles for the corners (E).

BLOCK ASSEMBLY

1. Select 4 pieced units and lay them out so that they form a donut shape around a C square.

2. Mark the ¼″ seamlines on the wrong side of the C square. Match the square and the inner sides of the pieced unit. Pin and then sew from corner to corner of C. Repeat for the opposite side and then the 2 remaining sides.

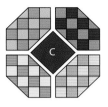

3. Fold the C square in half diagonally, as if you were mitering a border corner, and sew from the corners of C to the outside corners of the pieced units, to join all 4 outer seams to make a donut shape.

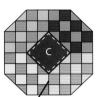

Sew from C out to join pieced units.

4. Repeat Steps 1–3 to make a total of 16 of these donuts.

QUILT ASSEMBLY

1. Following the quilt assembly diagram (below), place the donuts on the design wall in 4 rows of 4 donuts each. Fill in the inner gaps with the remaining C squares. Place D triangles along the gaps in the outer edges. Place an E triangle at each corner.

2. Sew the donuts, C squares, and D and E triangles together in diagonal rows as shown. See Sewing Y-Seams (below) to mark and pin the rows before stitching. When adding D and E triangles, be aware that you are sewing a bias edge. Pin and sew carefully.

3. Sew Row 1 to Row 2 and Row 6 to Row 7. Then join Rows 3 and 5 to Row 4. Then join the corner sections to the center section.

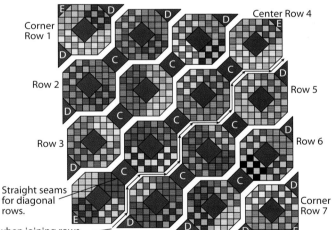

Quilt assembly diagram with Y-seams

sewing y-seams

Mark the corners of the D triangles, the C squares, and the donuts at the ¼″ seam allowance. Align the free side of a D triangle with the side of the first donut in the adjacent row. Pin through the marks at the first corner to align the first section of the 2 rows. Stitch slowly up to the pin and drop the needle into the hole as you pull the pin out. Lift the presser foot and bring the bottom layer of fabric into alignment with the top so that the raw edges of the next section of the seam are together. Pin through the marks at the corner at the end of this section. Drop the foot down and sew to the pin. Continue in this manner until you have completed joining the rows.

This easier assembly method avoids Y-seams but will have seams in the squares of inspiration fabric.

CUTTING

From inspiration fabric:

• Cut 8 strips 4⅞" × WOF. Subcut 64 squares 4⅞" × 4⅞"; subcut each square on the diagonal once to make 128 triangles for corner units (E).

BLOCK ASSEMBLY

Sew E triangles to the outside corners of each pieced unit to make 64 blocks.

Sew E triangles to corners of pieced unit.

QUILT ASSEMBLY

1. Lay the quilt out again in 8 rows of 8 blocks. Pin the blocks together at the joins and sew the blocks into rows.

2. Pin and sew the rows together to make the quilt center.

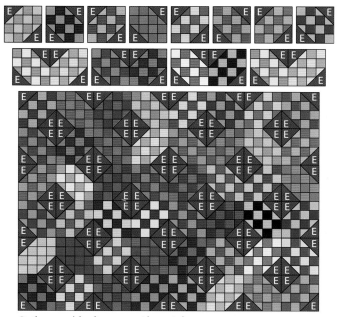

Quilt assembly diagram with straight-set rows

Borders

1. Cut 4 strips 10½" × 90" from border fabric.

2. Trace the appliqué shapes (pullout pages P1–P4) onto freezer paper.

3. Press the freezer paper, shiny side down, onto the right side of the fat quarter appliqué fabrics. Trace around the shapes with a chalk pencil.

4. Cut out with a scant ¼" seam allowance from the edge of the freezer paper and then peel it off. Finger-press the seam allowance to the back.

5. When you have all the shapes prepared, lay them out on the border strips as in the photo (page 35).

6. Use a glue pen to baste the shapes in place. Needle-turn appliqué them onto the border strips.

7. Refer to Mitered Corner Borders (page 33) to attach the borders.

8. Layer, baste, and quilt.

9. Cut 9 strips 2½" × WOF from the binding fabric. Join the 9 binding strips end to end with diagonal seams and use to bind the quilt.

Attaching Borders

When border strips are cut on the crosswise grain, piece the strips together to achieve the needed lengths.

This quilt was made with mitered borders, but you can choose to add butted borders instead.

Mitered Corner Borders

Measure the length of the quilt top and add two times the cut width of the border, plus 5″. This is the length you need to cut or piece the side borders.

Place pins at the centers of both side borders and all four sides of the quilt top. From the center pin, measure in both directions and mark half of the measured length of the quilt top on both side borders. Pin, matching the centers and the marked length of the side border to the edges of the quilt top. Stitch the strips to the sides of the quilt top by starting ¼″ in from the beginning edge of the quilt top, backstitching, and then continuing down the length of the side border. Stop stitching ¼″ before the ending edge of the quilt top, at the seam allowance line, and backstitch. The excess length of the side borders will extend beyond each edge. Press the seams toward the borders.

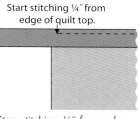

Start stitching ¼″ from edge of quilt top.

Stop stitching ¼″ from edge.

Determine the length needed for the top and bottom border the same way, measuring the width of the quilt top through the center including each side border. Add two times the cut width of the border plus 5″ to this measurement. Cut or piece the top and bottom border strips to this length. From the center of each border strip, measure in both directions and mark half the measured width of the quilt top. Again, pin and start and stop stitching at the previous stitching lines, ¼″ from the quilt edges, and backstitch. The border strips extend beyond each end. Press the seams toward the borders.

To create the miter, lay the corner on the ironing board. Working with the quilt right side up, lay one border strip on top of the adjacent border.

With right sides up, fold the top border strip under itself so that it meets the edge of the adjacent border and forms a 45° angle. Pin the fold in place.

Fold under at a 45° angle.

Position a 90° angle triangle or ruler over the corner to check that the corner is flat and square. When everything is in place, press the fold firmly.

Square corner

Remove the pins. Fold the center section of the top diagonally from the corner, right sides together, and align the long edges of the border strips. On the wrong side, place pins near the pressed fold in the corner to secure the border strips.

Beginning at the inside corner at the border seamline, stitch, backstitch, and then stitch along the fold toward the outside point of the border corners, being careful not to allow any stretching to occur. Backstitch at the end. Trim the excess border fabric to a ¼″ seam allowance. Press the seam open.

Wrong side of quilt

Stitch toward the outside edge.

Butted Borders

In most cases the side borders are sewn on first. When you have finished the quilt top, measure it through the center vertically. This will be the length to cut the side borders.

Place pins at the centers of all four sides of the quilt top, as well as in the center of each side border strip. Pin the side borders to the quilt top first, matching the center pins. Using a ¼″ seam allowance, sew the borders to the quilt top and press toward the border.

Measure horizontally across the center of the quilt top including the side borders. This will be the length to cut the top and bottom borders. Repeat, pinning, sewing, and pressing as you did for the side borders.

How I Finished

To quilt I used black perle cotton size 12. I quilted
diagonal lines through the squares and used a leaf and
flower pattern for each of the units. You can follow this
line by using the quilting pattern (pullout page P1),
or you can straight-line quilt along the squares, which
would also look good. When making stash quilts with
a lot of fabrics, it isn't always necessary to quilt a lot, as
the beauty of the quilt is in the fabric.

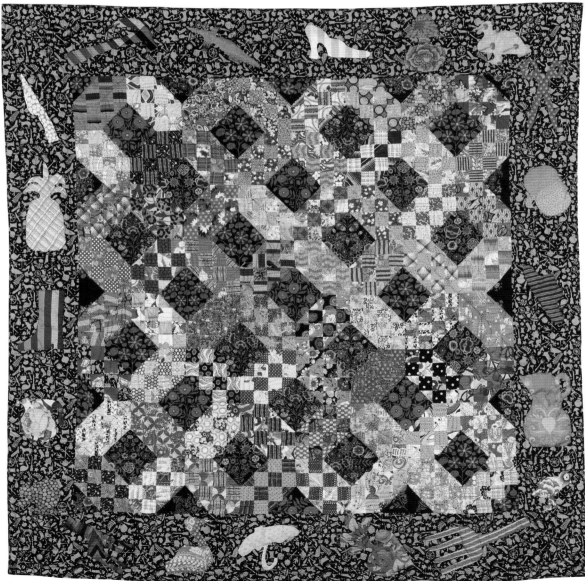

Fractured Heart

FINISHED QUILT: 84″ × 84″ (213cm × 213cm)

How I Started

Is there anything more impulsive than the excited beat of the heart? Young girls can react to affairs of the heart in an erratic manner. It's love. No, it isn't. ... Yes, it *is*! *Fractured Heart* symbolizes the impulsive nature of choices. The fabrics in this quilt are entirely from my stash and very impulsively chosen. The reds are primarily, but not exclusively, Kaffe Fassett. The thing is, Kaffe does red like no one else; and when I use his red, all the other colors look better. So when I was gathering fabrics for this quilt, that was where I started. The background nearly depleted my white base fabric collection! So just keep your reds red and have a bit of a play with the background neutrals and you can make this quilt your own in no time, one heartbeat at a time.

MATERIALS

*Yardage based on 42″ (107cm) usable WOF.**

BLOCKS AND BACKGROUND:

- 3⅝ yards (3.3m) total of light fabrics with hints of pink, orange, and red for background and heart blocks

- 2 yards (1.8m) total of red, dark pink, red/orange, and magenta fabrics for heart blocks

BORDER: 1¼ yards (1.2m)

BACKING: 8 yards (7.3m)

BINDING: ¾ yard (70cm)

BATTING: 92″ × 92″ (234cm × 234cm)

* WOF = width of fabric

CUTTING

From assorted light fabrics:

- Cut 29 strips 4½" × WOF. Set aside 16 strips for the heart blocks.

- From the remaining 13 strips, subcut 117 squares 4½" × 4½" for the background blocks and the V at the top of the heart.

From assorted heart fabrics:

- Cut 16 strips 4½" × WOF for the heart blocks.

From a heart fabric:

- Cut 2 squares 4½" × 4½" for the V at the top of the heart.

From another heart fabric:

- Cut 1 square 4½" × 4½" for the bottom point of the heart.

From border fabric:

- Cut 8 strips 4½" × WOF for the borders. Join them end to end into a continuous strip.

From binding fabric:

- Cut 9 strips 2½" × WOF.

Construction

All seam allowances are ¼" unless otherwise noted.

1. Make 16 pairs of 4½" × WOF strips of 1 background and 1 heart fabric. Both strips of fabric should be right side up; align the long edges carefully.

2. Subcut the pairs of strips at 5" intervals to yield 8 background and 8 heart rectangles 4½" × 5" from each pair of strips. You will need 121 rectangles each of background and heart fabric.

3. From each pair of rectangles, cut a vertical slice through the center at a slight angle. Swap the right-hand background and heart pieces to yield 2 light/dark sets from each pair of rectangles.

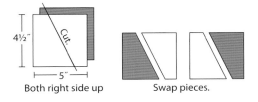

Both right side up   Swap pieces.

Adding Layers—Color, Design & Imagination

4. Flip the right-hand piece so the pieces are right sides together. Sew along the diagonal edges. Remember that the seam is on an angle, so the dog-ears should match at each end of the seam to adjust for the angle. The completed heart block should now be 4½″ × 4½″ square. Press and trim if needed. Repeat this process to make a total of 241 pieced heart blocks.

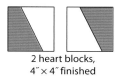

2 heart blocks,
4″ × 4″ finished

5. Place a 4½″ × 4½″ heart fabric square right side down on the left side of a 4½″ × 4½″ background square. Sew a diagonal seam from the top left corner to the bottom middle of the square. Trim ¼″ away from the seam as shown. Press open.

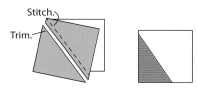

Stitch.

Trim.

6. Repeat Step 5 on the right-hand side of the background square to complete the joining square for the middle of the heart.

4″ × 4″ finished

Assembly

1. Refer to the photo or quilt assembly diagram and use your design wall to place the units accordingly, in 19 rows of 19 heart blocks or background squares. Pay attention to the orientation of the heart blocks, as they create the stair-stepped heart outlines.

tip

If you don't have a large design wall, follow the key below the quilt assembly diagram to arrange your blocks and squares in sections before assembling them.

Arrange into 2 sections that are 9 units by 10 rows and 2 that are 10 units by 10 rows.

2. When the units are all in place to your liking, sew them together in rows by section.

3. Join the top 2 sections together and then the bottom 2, and then sew the top and bottom halves together to complete the quilt top center.

4. Refer to Butted Borders (page 34) to measure the quilt top center, trim the border strip into 2 strips 4½″ × 76½″ for the sides and 2 strips 4½″ × 84½″ for the top and bottom (adjust your measurements if needed), and attach them to the quilt top center.

5. Layer, baste, and quilt. Join the 9 binding strips end to end with diagonal seams and use them to bind the quilt.

Quilt assembly diagram

(**Key:** B = background square; H = heart block; V = joining square; R = red square)

How I Finished

Grace Widders machine quilted this quilt on a domestic machine ½″ outside the seamlines to reinforce the linear pattern. As an alternative, it could easily be hand quilted with perle cotton size 8. An allover continuous pattern could work, too, if desired.

Follow the Sun

How I Started

Oftentimes a single fabric will bring an entire collection of stash fabrics together into one happy quilt. Such is the case with *Follow the Sun*. The Anastasia fabric by Alexander Henry arrived, and we all jumped on it, literally pulling the bolt out of each other's hands! The colors are fantastic and the design is great for fussy cutting, but for me, the colorful graphic floral trailing in vertical paths up the length of the fabric shouted, "Cut me into sashing strips!" So it was done. I cut a long length of the fabric into four strips 6½″ wide and put them on the design wall. The gray spot had just enough energy to sit back quietly yet still command a bit of notice. Now I had a stack of fabric strips, but what should I do with them?

The element of chance played a strong role here. The acrylic templates for a favorite block of mine, the Queen of the May, were already out, being used to make sample blocks. So in a very natural way the fabric and template came together and the blocks were born. I wanted to showcase some of the bigger-print fabrics in my stash, so I decided to use only the outer ring of the block. The outside ring was fun to coordinate with the large fussy cutting of the circle centers. In the end, this quilt came together with ease.

MATERIALS

Yardage based on 42″ (107cm) usable WOF.*

RED DIRECTIONAL PRINT:
- 3½ yards (3.2m) for sashing
- 1¾ yards (1.6m) for star points

24 DIFFERENT GRAPHIC PRINTS:
- ⅛ yard (10cm) each of 12 fabrics for inner circle points
- ⅛ yard (10cm) each of 12 fabrics for outer circle points

12 DIFFERENT EXCITING FEATURE PRINTS:
- 1 fat quarter of each for circle centers

GRAY/BLACK SPOT: 3 yards (2.8m) for background

MUSLIN: ¾ yard (70cm) for star block assembly

NARROW RICKRACK: 13½ yards (12.3m)

BACKING: 7½ yards (6.9m)

BINDING: ¾ yard (70cm)

BATTING: 86″ × 95″ (220cm × 240cm)

OPTIONAL TOOLS AND TEMPLATES:
- Acrylic Queen of the May template set from Material Obsession
- 8½″ circle template or rotary circle cutter

* WOF = width of fabric

CUTTING

Sashing:

From red fabric:

- *Vertical strips:* Cut 4 strips 6½″ × 81½″ *on the lengthwise grain of the fabric* for the vertical sashing strips. The remaining fabric can be used for star points.

- *Horizontal strips:* Cut 9 strips 3½″ × WOF. Set aside 4 of these strips for the top and bottom borders. Subcut the remaining WOF strips to make 9 strips 3½″ × 18½″ for the horizontal sashing strips.

Set the sashing and border strips aside.

Stars:

From red fabric:

- Cut 28 squares 5½″ × 5½″ from the remaining vertical sashing fabric for the star points.

- Cut another 10 strips 5½″ × WOF; subcut 68 squares 5½″ × 5½″ for the star points.

You need a total of 96 squares for the star points.

Background:

From gray/black spot fabric:

- Cut 18 strips 5½″ × WOF; subcut 48 rectangles 5½″ × 8½″ and 48 squares 5½″ × 5½″.

From muslin:

- Cut 3 strips 8½″ × WOF; subcut 12 squares 8½″ × 8½″.

- Make 12 sets of 4 spot rectangles, 4 spot squares, 8 red star point squares, and 1 muslin square and set aside.

Pieced circle borders:

From each of 24 different graphic prints:

Note: If you are using the Material Obsession Queen of the May acrylic template set, use the C template for the inner circle points and the D template for the outer circle points. You will not need the A and B templates from this set to make *Follow the Sun.*

Each triangle will be on a unique graphic print, according to this design. Your own design could be different!

1. Cut a strip of fabric 3¼″ × WOF for the inner circle points.

2. Cut a strip of fabric 2¾″ × WOF for the outer circle points.

3. If you are copying the patterns (next page) onto template plastic, trace with a fine pencil or pen around the outside of the inner point pattern onto a repeated motif on the fabric. Trace and cut 12 inner points from a graphic print fabric.

4. Trace and cut 12 outer point pieces from a graphic print fabric. This piece is not fussy cut, so you can rotate the template to optimize your fabric use.

5. Repeat Steps 1–4 to cut a total of 12 sets of 12 inner and 12 outer circle points.

If you have acrylic templates cut to shape, follow the directions in the photos to cut 12 sets of 12 inner point and 12 outer point triangles from your graphic print fabrics.

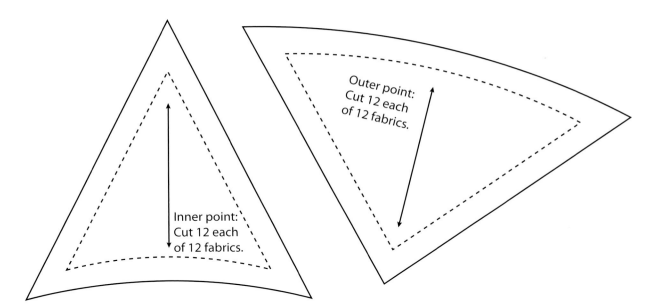

Inner point:
Cut 12 each
of 12 fabrics.

Outer point:
Cut 12 each
of 12 fabrics.

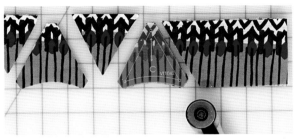

Cut a width-of-fabric strip that is the height of the inner circle point template. These pieces are fussy cut across the strip by placing the template in the same direction, on the same portion of the print each time. That way the design of the fabric stays the same for each piece.

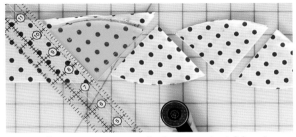

Cut template D using a second ruler to cut the left-hand side. Here fussy cutting is not required, so you can flip the template across the strip to optimize fabric use.

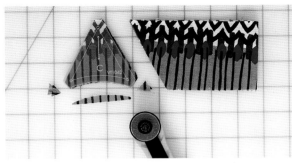

Using a small-blade rotary cutter makes cutting the curves easier. Be sure to trim the tips, which will make sewing easier.

Circle centers:

- Using an 8½″ circle template, a rotary circle cutter, or a compass and scissors, cut out 12 really fabulous center circles from the fat quarters.

Note: It isn't essential to center the design perfectly in the circle, and, in fact, it will be more interesting if the design is slightly off center.

Binding:

- From the binding fabric, cut 9 strips 2½″ × WOF.

Sewing

All seam allowances are ¼" unless otherwise noted.

1. Make 12 pairs of combined inner and outer point triangles (cut from the patterns or templates). Mark the seamlines with a ¼" ruler and sew them together on a machine or by hand along the straight edges.

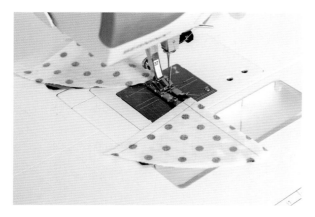

2. Continue joining the pairs in the same manner until you have a circle. Press it flat, with all the seams going in the same direction.

Join pairs of alternating shapes.

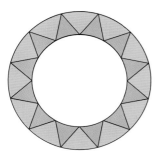

3. Fold the center circle in half and then in quarters like a pie. Press the folds to mark the segments in the circle. With the pieced circle on top and both circles right sides together, match the creases to the seams in the outer circle. Pin through all 12 seams.

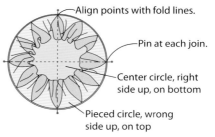

Align points with fold lines.

Pin at each join.

Center circle, right side up, on bottom

Pieced circle, wrong side up, on top

4. With the pieced circle wrong side up on top, machine sew ¼" from the edge around the circle and through each point. Sew slowly and be sure *not* to crease the center circle fabric into the seam. If you do, unpick and resew the seam. Press flat.

5. Repeat Steps 1–4 with the remaining sets of inner and outer circle pieces and 8½" circles to make a total of 12 pieced circle units.

STAR BLOCKS

For each star you will need 4 gray/black spot corners, 4 gray/black spot rectangles, 8 red star points, and a muslin square, which you set aside earlier.

1. Fold the red squares in half on the diagonal and finger-press. Place the square so the edges line up with the gray rectangles. Sew along the creased diagonal line. Trim away ¼" on the outside seam. Fold open and press the triangle to fill the corner.

2. Repeat Step 1 on the other side of the gray rectangle.

Sew along diagonal fold line.

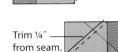

Trim ¼" from seam.

3. Repeat Steps 1 and 2 to make a total of 48 pieced units.

Trim ¼" from seam.

4. Join pieced units to opposite sides of the muslin square as shown to make the center row of the block.

5. Join a black/gray spot square to each side of a pieced unit as shown to make the top row. Repeat to make the bottom row.

6. Join the 3 rows together as per the diagram.

Repeat Steps 4–6 to make a total of 12 stars.

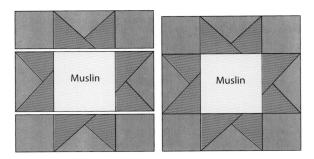

STAR APPLIQUÉ

You will need 40" of rickrack for each circle. This is a popular method for joining circles to backgrounds, as there are no raw edges.

1. Lay the rickrack on the right side of the pieced circle, aligned with the raw edge of the circle and with about 1" to spare at each end.

2. Stitch the rickrack in place ¼" away from the edge of the circle, through the center of the rickrack.

Note: If you go slow and steady, there is no need to pin. Ease the rickrack in as you go.

3. When you are near the starting point, stop sewing and work the rickrack so that the hills overlap. Fold the end up toward the middle of the circle, away from the raw edge, and sew the end under. Trim off any excess at the beginning of the rickrack.

4. Fold the raw edges of the pieced circle to the wrong side and press in place to get a nice finished edge. Press evenly to ensure that you have a flat seam to sew and even hills and valleys.

5. Pin the circle, right side up, to the center of the star block so that only the star points show. Sew along the previous stitching line on the rickrack to secure in place.

6. Repeat Steps 1–5 for each block.

Assembly

1. Refer to the quilt assembly diagram (below) to lay the blocks out in 3 columns of 4 star blocks and 3 red 3½″ × 18½″ sashing strips each, starting and finishing with blocks. Join the star blocks and sashing strips together in columns.

2. Sew the columns together with the 4 red 6½″ × 81½″ sashing strips, starting and finishing with the sashing strips. *Make sure to orient the print in the same direction for all of them.*

joining sashing and borders

It is essential when joining long sashing strips to first find the center of each sashing strip and pieced row. Match and pin the centers and then the ends, which should be equal lengths, and pin evenly throughout. If the sashing strips are longer or shorter than the pieced strips, ease or stretch gently and evenly to make the strips fit, easing or stretching evenly throughout the distance of the join.

3. Join 4 of the red 3½″ × WOF strips together end to end and trim to make 2 lengths, each 3½″ × 78½″, for the top and bottom borders.

4. Matching the centers and the ends as in Step 2, sew the top and bottom borders to the quilt.

5. Layer, baste, and quilt. Join the 9 binding strips end to end with diagonal seams and use them to bind the quilt.

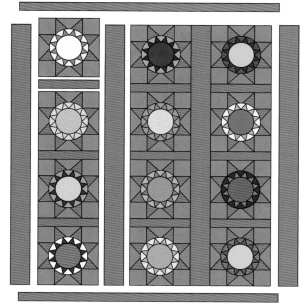

Quilt assembly diagram

How I Finished

For this quilt I wanted to treat the blocks differently than the sashing strips, which are quilted with black perle cotton size 12 in long, trailing vines with soft leaves. I used a chalk pencil and freehand drew the lines so that they were continuous along the length. I used black to be consistent throughout the quilt and to not overshadow the variety of colors. For the pieced blocks, the backgrounds are stabilized with taupe thread to match the spot background. The centers of the circles are quilted with straight lines that connect the outer points in a variety of colors. The freehand style means that it is easy to pick up the project at any time and carry on with the quilting in a no-fuss manner.

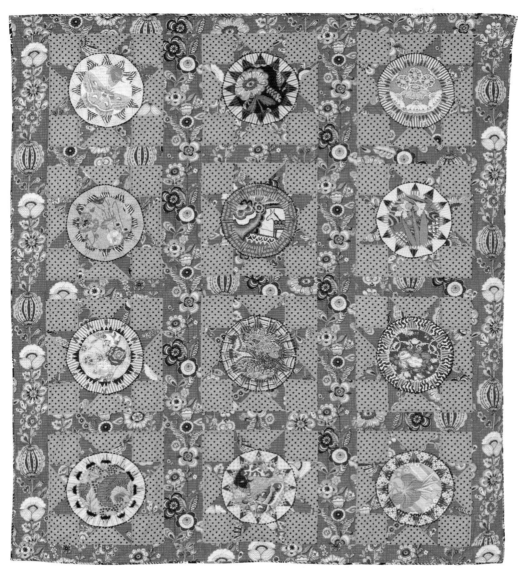

Madness

FINISHED QUILT: 68″ × 82″ (173cm × 208cm)

How I Started

Stash quilts are by nature a great way to express yourself. You may like organized patterns that have structure and definitive lines. Or you may like lines all over the place that reflect an impulsive, eclectic nature. *Madness* is the latter of the two styles. The original inspiration came from the marvelous Anna Williams, one of my favorite African-American quilters. Anna pieced seemingly random pieces of fabric into delightful collections of outrageous color. This style appears to have little structure, but don't be fooled. It takes concentration to make a quilt like this. It takes a lot of time, thoughtfulness, and strip piecing. But none of it is hard; the tricks are in the process.

When making a stash quilt it is important to use fabrics that relate to each other well because they live in the same family. Group the fabrics into clean white-based colors or tonal colors. The amount of white in a fabric determines how it moves forward. Uneven use of white versus tonal fabrics can make the quilt confusing. If you have a lot of scraps that are more country style, you might want to consider adjusting the black and white to dark brown or even red strips to make order with less conflict.

The black and white spots, stripes, patterns, and graphic prints work to add linear definition to the variety of prints, shapes, and colors in this quilt. Take them away and it is a real mess. If you are making a quilt that is more tonal (country colors), you may want to use brown or gray instead of black and white.

When I started this quilt I gathered all my orphan blocks, sample blocks, and leftover sashings. Then I went through my scrap basket and cut all the strips into strips of varying widths. I hung them on hangers in warm and color groups. That way when I was ready to get started, it was easy.

MATERIALS

*Yardage based on 42″ (107cm) usable WOF.**

FABRICS:

- ⅓ yard (30cm) each of 5–7 black-and-white prints that vary from white-on-black to black-on-white, spots, stripes, and decorative designs

- Strips of fabric 1½″–3″ wide (These can be joined in alternating colors—generally warm/cool or light/dark.)

- Collection of made fabric, scraps, and odd or orphan blocks or practice pieces

For the quilt as photographed:

BACKING: 5⅛ yards (4.7m)

BINDING: ⅝ yard (60cm)

BATTING: 76″ × 90″ (195cm × 230cm)

* WOF = *width of fabric*

Preparation

Keep these ideas in mind as you go:

- As often as possible, sew alternating warm and cool color patterns when joining scraps together.

- Use black and white to break up the flow of the colors and to add definition to the shape of the quilt.

- If the strips, blocks, or pieces are too big, trim them back; and if they are too small, add a bit to make them fit.

- Start with a few blocks made up and use your design wall to create balance and to decipher where patterns are appearing.

- Even though it hurts, cut into large bits and interrupt the flow!

- Square up the blocks and sections as the quilt grows.

- At the end, toss the remaining bits and *move on*!

- Don't sweat the technique. Have fun. . . .

This pattern is written as a "recipe" without specific sizes. The idea is that in the process of making it you learn to see what you are looking at and how to construct that piece. It is a great opportunity to find lines, decipher block construction, and take matters into your own hands—even if it makes you a little crazy!

Have a long look at the photo and try to define the 3 sections inside the borders. When you see them, start with the top section and add strips or blocks until you have the width that you require. Set the top section aside and start making the middle section in the same manner until it is the same width as the top. If it is too big, trim it back, or if it is too small, simply add another section to make it fit. Work the third section in the same way and then join all 3 sections together.

Build this quilt in sections. Establish the width of the quilt with the first section and then grow the next sections to fit. Make the side borders to fit your chosen sides.

note

It is important that you square up each section as you go along. If you don't, the quilt will not lie flat. Keep in mind that when you are sewing sections of the quilt together, the straight seams should be equal lengths. Measure each section through the middle and trim to fit. Then pin the middle and the two ends before sewing the sections together.

The first section is made with sections of sewn strips—some with diagonal interruptions, some just strips of shapes such as triangles, squares, and diamonds. It is always possible to increase the size of the blocks by adding a fabric strip and trimming to fit. These pieces can be anything, but if the quilt is looking busy, use black-and-white fabrics to define the sections.

Sections 2 and 3 can be made up of anything from leftover strips to random shapes. In the third section, the middle block was a leftover Log Cabin block. It would appear more obvious, but I cut it in quarters and pieced in additional strips to make it fit into the general feel of the quilt.

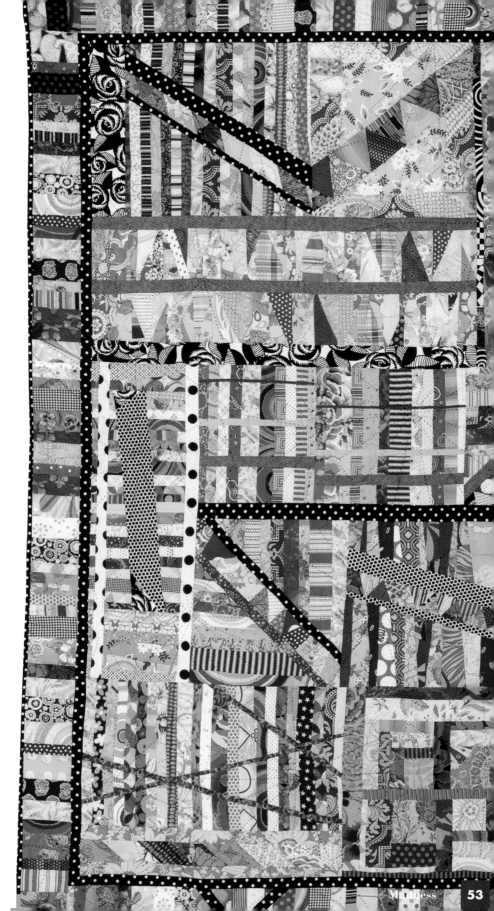

ELEMENTS TO INCLUDE

When we make quilts we often have the opportunity to use leftover pieces from other quilts. Sometimes there were just extra pieces and sometimes the color didn't work; maybe you made a bad cut or maybe you simply changed your mind about something. This is a great opportunity to use all those strips, squares, Flying Geese, half-square triangles, and 60° triangles. Sew similar shapes together into strips.

Collect unused strips from previous projects and use them!

Another option is to simply make fabric by sewing strips of fabric together along the length.

note

When sewing the strips together, trim them all to be the same length.

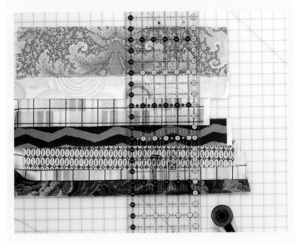

Try using your made fabric to make more Log Cabin blocks, Star blocks, or square-in-a-square units, or, if you are very ambitious, try hexagons.

Fill in empty spaces.

Experiment with the blocks on your design wall to get a visual image of where you are going and fill in the spaces as required. Some pieces may stay and some may go.

DIAGONAL CUTS

When the made fabric or blocks are ready, use a ruler set at an angle and cut through the piece. I know this sounds hard, but just do it! When the fabric is cut, it is then possible to insert pieced strips or just a length of fabric. Join the strip to one side of the diagonal seam. Gently press flat and then join the other side of this block—or, dare I say, even another block! Remember when sewing diagonal strips that you need to allow for the angle of the seam, so there should be at least the same size dog-ears on either end of the seams. When the seams are joined, trim the block to be square.

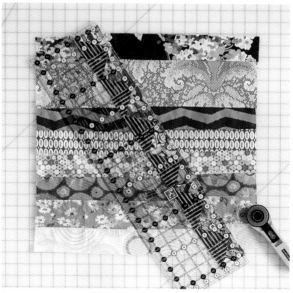

Position a ruler on the pieced strip and then cut on the diagonal.

Audition sets of strips to be sure you like them together. Place a long pieced strip diagonally on one of your pieced strip sets.

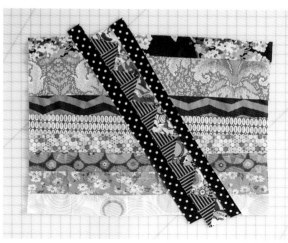

It is possible to use only the pieced strip on the diagonal, but note the difference when it is outlined by the black-and-white spot fabric. The spot clearly adds definition to the lines and makes it easier to see what is going on. By auditioning we see clearly the effect of the black-and-white spot, which is more exciting.

Assembly

All seam allowances are ¼" unless otherwise noted.

Build the quilt in 3 sections. Work until you have the width you like. Then make another section to that width. Keep working and adding sections to the quilt until it is the size you want. If the sections are too small, you can add in a piece of fabric to make up the difference.

INNER BORDER

These black-and-white spot fabric borders are great for adding definition and a sense of space and for squaring up the quilt, so it is essential to do this properly. Refer to Butted Borders (page 34) to measure the quilt top, cut the border strips, and sew them to the quilt top.

OUTER BORDER

The outer border is made up of scrap strips. The width of this border is up to you. Measure your quilt again to determine the required length of the side borders and top and bottom borders.

Simply join the lengths of scrap strips until you have enough. Keep going as long as you are having fun. Enjoy! Refer again to Butted Borders (page 34) to attach the outer borders.

After the borders are in place, layer, baste, and quilt.

BINDING

Cut as many strips 2½" × WOF as needed to equal the perimeter of your quilt, plus at least 18" extra. Sew the strips together end to end and use to bind your quilt.

How I Finished

I hand quilted this one using black perle cotton size 8.
I made freehand lines in circle shapes randomly
over the quilt, which further enhanced the scrappy,
devil-may-care feel of the project. However, a freehand
version of a Baptist Fan pattern would also work well
here. It's great for scrap quilts.

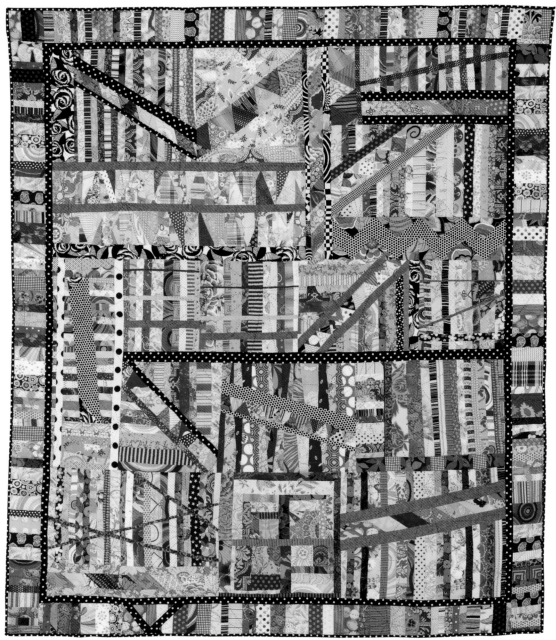

CHAPTER 2
Working with Templates

I don't have time! Well, I do, but there are a lot of demands on my time. So when I want to do something, I want to do it in the best, most efficient manner possible so that I don't *waste* time. That and a hate affair with math made me search for easy methods to cut and sew accurately. The result: I love templates. I use them all the time to cut straight lines, curves, hexagons, or multiple pieces accurately—and fast. The quilts in this section break down the mystery of a few of my favorite tools.

The instructions are written for traditional cutting methods, but I recommend trying the suggested templates. They make cutting accurate and repeatable. Once cut, the shapes are easy to sew accurately. The result: a well-made quilt that looks like you took the care to get a good result.

Heart Center

How I Started

Alexander Henry is a great source of dynamic, colorful, imaginative fabric collections that offer me an opportunity to play and to use my imagination. In this particular case, the starting point was the Madonna fabric. I have always loved the Madonna as a symbol of hope, faith, honesty, and femininity. So, with my handy-dandy 10° wedge ruler, I started cutting. I found I could fussy cut the Madonna to feature in some of the blades, and from the remaining fabric I could fussy cut some flowers. The alternating strips were random warm and cool solid colors that I had on hand that day

for the strip blades. The red star background is from an Anna Griffith Christmas line. The strips are evenly spaced, so they add great rhythm to the background. Other options are possible, from a solid to a stripe or even a magnificent large-scale floral. It is a simple quilt and fun to make—but be sure to pin the blades in order! I got a phone call while sewing my blades together and got it all messed up by sewing the left side of the pair instead of the right. And it makes a big difference. I had to go back and unpick it all and try again. … Live and learn!

MATERIALS   *Yardage based on 42″ (107cm) usable WOF.**

BACKGROUND:
4⅝ yards (4.3m)

• Choose a light background with an evenly spaced regular pattern.

FEATURE PRINT:
1⅓ yards (1.3m)

• Check that you can fussy cut 9 matching wedges from this amount of fabric. Depending on the pattern repeat, you might need more. If you are not fussy cutting, it is possible to cut 13 wedges from selvage to selvage if your fabric is not a directional print, so you would only need ⅔ yard.

STRIPE: ⅔ yard (65cm)

SOLIDS:

• ¼ yard (25cm) each of 2 different dark solid fabrics (or 2 strips each 2½″ × WOF)

• ⅛ yard (10cm) each of 10 different cool solid fabrics (or 1 strip each 2½″ × WOF)

• ⅛ yard (10cm) each of 10 different warm solid fabrics (or 1 strip each 2½″ × WOF)

Select colors that match your inspiration fabric. Some colors may work as both warm and cool, depending on the neighboring colors. I used the dark colors to define the outer edge of the circle against the background. The colors I used

are midnight blue, plum, navy, cobalt blue, dark green, light green, taupe, dark purple, tan, lavender, black, dark blue, dusty pink, light red, dark red, light plum, coral, and true red.

RED: Fat quarter for heart

BACKING: 7⅝ yards (7m)

BINDING: ⅝ yard (55cm)

BATTING: 88″ × 88″ (225cm × 225cm)

TOOLS: 10° wedge ruler, 22½″ long (that will make a 50″-diameter circle), or pattern provided (pullout page P1)

FREEZER PAPER: For appliqué

* WOF = width of fabric

Preparation

All seam allowances are ¼″ unless otherwise noted.

SOLID STRIP SETS

1. Cut each dark solid into 2 strips 2½″ × WOF.

2. Cut each warm and cool solid into 1 strip 2½″ × WOF.

> ### tip
> When sewing strips, trim all the same length.

3. Lay out a set of 10 warm solid strips, starting and finishing with a dark solid strip.

Use the colors as specified or make your own combinations. Each color set starts and ends with an equally dark value to give the finished circle a definitive edge.

4. Mark and then match the middle of each strip in pairs. Pin along the length, right sides together.

5. Sew the strips together in pairs. Continue sewing pairs together until you have a set of 12 strips. Press all the seams in one direction without stretching the fabric.

6. Repeat Steps 3–5 with the cool solid and remaining dark strips to make 1 cool strip set.

Cutting

WEDGES

1. Cut 1 strip each 22½″ × WOF from the feature print fabric and the striped fabric.

Refer to Cutting Wedges from Strips (page 15) to subcut the following, using the wedge ruler or a template made from the pattern (pullout page P1):

- 9 wedges of feature print fabric (I fussy cut 2 different designs, 5 of one and 4 of another.)
- 9 wedges of stripe fabric

2. Using a wedge ruler or the template from the previous step, cut 9 wedges each across the width of the warm and cool strip sets. *Note:* The strip sets should measure 24½″ high. Cut the first wedge with the wide end of the template at the top of the strip set; then rotate the template so that the second wedge has the wide end at the bottom. The wide outside edge will always show and needs to be equal, so always place it even with the edge of the strip set. The narrow end will be covered by the heart.

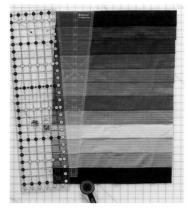

Use the 10° wedge ruler to cut the wedges. Position the ruler and cut along the right side. Bring in a second ruler and cut along the left.

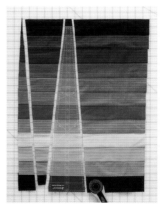

Rotate the template to cut the next wedge.

HEART

1. Fold the red fat quarter in half, *wrong sides together*, through the longer side.

2. Trace the heart pattern (pullout page P1) or roughly draw half a heart on freezer paper.

Cut out the shape and press the shiny side of the freezer paper onto the right side of the fabric, aligning the straight edge with the fold. Trace the outside of the shape with a chalk pencil, making sure to trace on both sides of the fold. Cut out the heart with your preferred seam allowance for needle-turn appliqué.

3. Remove the freezer paper and finger-press along the inside of the chalk pencil line so that the raw edge folds over to the back. The finger-pressing will make it easy to appliqué the heart to the center of the circle later.

BINDING

Cut 8 strips 2½″ × WOF of binding fabric.

Assembly

1. Using your design wall, place all the blades in a circle, alternating the feature print and striped fabric with the pieced blades. Remember that the pieced blades alternate both warm and cool colors and top-to-bottom orientation.

Note: It is a good idea to photograph the layout and then pin the blades in pairs. Avoid the mess I mentioned earlier!

2. When the wedges are laid out and the orientation is secure, sew them together from the outside edge to the center. Keep in mind that the outer seams will show, while the inner circle will be covered by the heart.

3. When the circle is complete, fold it in half both horizontally and vertically. Finger-press or use your iron to mark the quarter lines.

4. Fold the heart in half both horizontally and vertically. Finger-press or iron to mark the creases.

5. Place the heart on the pieced circle, matching the creases, and pin or glue-baste in place.

6. Needle-turn appliqué the heart in place.

7. Cut the background fabric into 2 equal lengths. Trim the selvages. Join the pieces carefully down the length, matching the pattern if necessary and using a ½″ seam allowance.

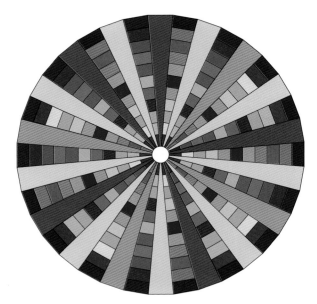

Circle assembly from wedges

Another Look

A while back I was fascinated with the recurring design elements of patchwork in other cultures. *Culture Blend* was made to reflect the Aboriginal art of native Australians. The fabrics are from Aboriginal artists. The quilt has a circle at the center that radiates outward. I thought about the warm colors of the earth, allowing for hits of dusty sun rays, and created the designs on linen for an earthy feel. Often the Aboriginal painters have animal tracks in their paintings; I used squiggly lines in the quilting to bring the trails to life on the background. Although *Culture Blend* uses the same techniques as *Heart Center*, it has a completely different effect.

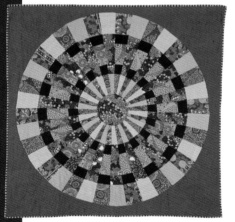

tip

If your background requires pattern matching, fold and press ½" to the wrong side along the length of 1 piece. Place the pieces one on top of the other, right sides together with the folded edge up, on a large flat surface. Using the visible portion of the pattern, match the top to the bottom and pin in place, leaving a ½" seam allowance on the lower piece.

8. Fold the joined background in half both horizontally and vertically to make quarters and press to mark the creases. Unfold. Place the circle on the background, matching the creases, and pin or baste securely in place. The wedges have straight ends, but when they are sewn together, the ¼" seam forms a circle easily. You may mark the ¼" seam allowance along the outer edge before needle-turning in place for an accurate curve. Use a ruler and a chalk pencil to mark ¼" at 1" intervals around the outside edge. Finger-press the fabric along the marks to the back and then pin in place. Needle-turn appliqué the circle in place on a large flat surface.

9. Trim the quilt top to 80½" × 80½" unfinished.

Done! That is the top!

10. Layer, baste, and quilt. Join the 8 binding strips end to end with diagonal seams and use them to bind the quilt.

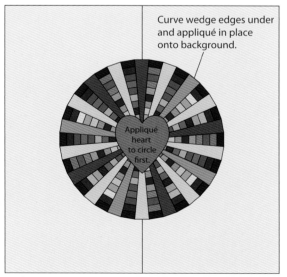

Curve wedge edges under and appliqué in place onto background.

Appliqué heart to circle first.

Quilt assembly diagram

How I Finished

I decided to use QuiltLite, which is a very lightweight cotton batting sold in Australia that is similar in weight to flannel. It makes it a nice summer-weight quilt.

Grace Widders quilted the quilt on a domestic machine. We discussed the project and agreed that a minimum amount of quilting would suffice; we decided to follow the rays of the blades from the heart center out to the edges. Hand quilting accentuates the heart.

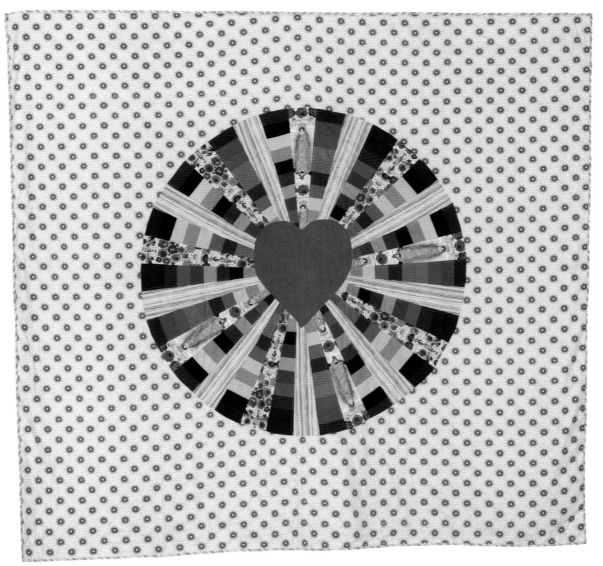

Ikat Diamonds

FINISHED QUILT: 65″ × 70″ (165cm × 178cm)

How I Started

The myriad of tribal-style textiles and geometric patterns originating from the cultural history of Asia and the Middle East are a rich source of inspiration. The Reece Scannell shot cottons are a weave of two colors that create a lustrous appeal and work beautifully with the woven ikat fabric. The real impact of the quilt results from the almost random coordination of light and dark values in the pieced borders, which is achieved by pairing the solids with varying degrees of value variation. At some of the corner junctions a random color is thrown in to interrupt the flow of the pattern, creating subtle, unexpected interest.

MATERIALS   *Yardage based on 42″ (107cm) usable WOF.**

IKAT FABRIC OR FEATURE FABRIC: ¾ yard (70cm) each of red, dark blue, orange, purple, yellow, and light blue fabrics or a total of 4½ yards (4.2m) for diamond blocks

SHOT COTTONS: 2½ yards (2.3m) total of light and dark solid fabrics (equal amount of lights and darks—I used 19 different colors, some of which I used as both light and dark, depending on the combination: white, gray, beige, pale lavender, gold, light pink, yellow-green, fuchsia, brown, teal, bright pink, dark red, dark brown, navy, plum, dark lavender, rust, purple, dark orange, and purple) for triangle sashing strips

BACKING: 4⅛ yards (3.8m)

BINDING: ⅝ yard (60cm)

BATTING: 72″ × 78″ (185cm × 200cm)

OPTIONAL TOOLS:

- 60° diamond template for 12″-high finished diamond

- 60° triangle ruler for 6″-high finished triangle

- 60° Strip Ruler for Triangles (by Creative Grids)

- Alternatively, use template plastic to make templates from patterns (pullout page P1).

* WOF = width of fabric

tips

- I recommend the Creative Grids strip rulers for multiples of shapes that can be cut from 2½″-wide strips. They are quick and accurate and make light work of repetition, considering the large quantity of small triangles. Otherwise, you can cut the triangles individually with the flat-tip triangle pattern provided. The other important thing to note is that the flat tip helps keep the straight-grain edge identified when sewing, for a better result.

- *Watch out!* Triangles have a lot of bias, so be sure that you cut according to the straight-grain arrows in the diagrams. The diamonds should have opposing straight-grain sides to help keep the sashing strips straight.

CUTTING

Diamond blocks:

- From feature fabrics, cut 16 strips 6½″ × WOF. Subcut the following using the patterns provided (pullout page P1) or your own templates: 67 diamonds and 16 equilateral (60°) triangles.

- From remaining feature fabrics, cut 2 strips 4″ × WOF (or use scraps, but be aware of the grain of the fabric). Subcut 10 long half-diamonds using your diamond template or the pattern (pullout page P1).

Be sure to cut the shapes from various colors. This may require an extra WOF strip or 2.

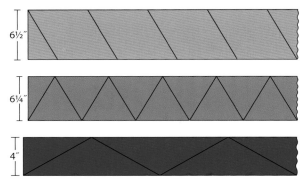

Cut each shape as shown with regard to the straight grain of the fabric.

Sashing:

- Cut 28 total strips 2½″ × WOF from the solid fabrics (14 light and 14 dark).

- Refer to Using Special Rulers: 60° (Equilateral) Triangles (page 17) to use the Creative Grids 60° strip ruler to subcut pairs of 60° triangles from pairs of the light and dark 2½″ × WOF strips. *Leave the pairs together as they were cut for ease of sewing later.*

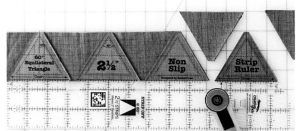

Use the Creative Grids strip ruler and pairs of 2½″ × WOF strips to cut multiples of the small 60° triangles.

- Or use the sashing triangle pattern (pullout page P1) to cut pairs, rotating the template with each cut.

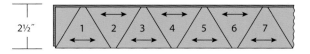

You will need a total of 260 pairs of light and dark triangles, plus 5 single triangles to complete the side rows (525 total). Each WOF strip should yield 23 sashing triangles.

Binding:

- Cut 7 strips 2½″ × WOF.

Sewing

All seam allowances are ¼" unless otherwise noted.

BLOCK ASSEMBLY

Refer to the quilt assembly diagram (page 71) to arrange all the cut diamonds, large triangles, and long half-diamonds on your design wall or a large flat area. Follow the finished quilt photo (page 73) for color placement, or play around with the pieces until you are happy with the balance. Be careful not to stretch any bias edges out of shape as you move the pieces. Gently move groups of pieces off the wall and sew them into blocks as detailed on this page.

1. Sew 2 diamonds together into a diagonal row as shown. Repeat to make a second row. Sew the 2 rows together to make a diamond block. Repeat to make a total of 14 diamond blocks.

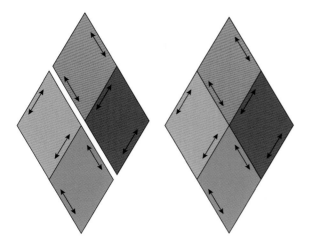

2. Sew a large triangle to 2 adjacent sides of a diamond as shown to make a triangle block. Make sure the straight-grain edges of the triangles (the edge opposite the blunt tip) are along the base of the block. Repeat this step to make a total of 7 triangle blocks.

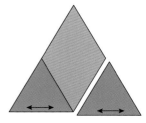

3. Sew long half-diamonds to 2 adjacent sides of a diamond as shown to make a half-diamond block. Make sure the straight-grain edges of the triangles (the edge opposite the blunt tip) are along the long side of the block. Repeat this step to make a total of 4 half-diamond blocks.

4. Sew a long half-diamond to a large triangle as shown to make a corner block as shown. Repeat this step to make 1 reversed corner block as shown.

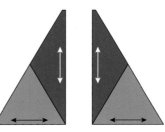

SASHING STRIPS

The seemingly random placement of lights and darks in this quilt is an important design element. The illustrations here and the quilt assembly diagram (page 71) present a straight-forward way to assemble the pieced sashing strips. It is possible to follow the diagram exactly, but if you would like to add an element of chance and a bit more interest, make equal value substitutions in some of the sets and at the junctions.

1. Refer to Using Special Rulers (pages 16 and 17) to sew the pairs of light and dark sashing triangles together along a bias edge, keeping the pairs together as they were cut and feeding pairs into the sewing machine with the blunt tip first. Press the unit open. The straight grain should run along the top and bottom of the paired unit. Repeat this step to make a total of 260 sewn pairs.

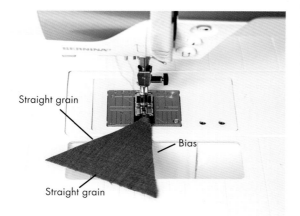

Straight grain

Bias

Straight grain

2. Join 6 matching sewn triangle pairs into a 6-pair sashing strip. Be sure to join the pairs along the bias edges again, so that the long sides of the sashing strip will be on the straight grain. Press and trim off the dog-ears. Repeat this step to make a total of 20 sashing strips.

3. Join 7 sewn triangle pairs into a 7-pair sashing strip. Press and trim off the dog-ears. Repeat this step to make a total of 20 sashing strips.

4. Put the completed blocks back up on your design wall. Arrange the 6-pair sashing rows between blocks as shown in the quilt assembly diagram (page 71). Arrange the 7-pair sashing strips in long diagonal rows between the diagonal rows of blocks. Play with the sashing strip placement so that the colors float. Be sure that the lightest colors and the darkest colors are evenly balanced among the strips. Stop, step back, and look at it; move anything that holds or stops your eye.

Assembly

1. When you are happy with the layout, sew the diamond blocks, triangle blocks, half-diamond blocks, and corner blocks into diagonal rows, with the 6-pair sashing strips between the blocks.

2. Sew the 7-pair sashing strips end to end into sashing rows as shown.

3. Sew single sashing triangles to 1 end of 4 of the long sashing rows and 1 of the 6-pair sashing strips as shown in the diagram.

4. Pin the long sashing rows to the block rows and sew all the rows together to complete the quilt top, taking care to match the points.

5. Layer, baste, and quilt. Join the 7 binding strips end to end with diagonal seams and use them to bind the quilt.

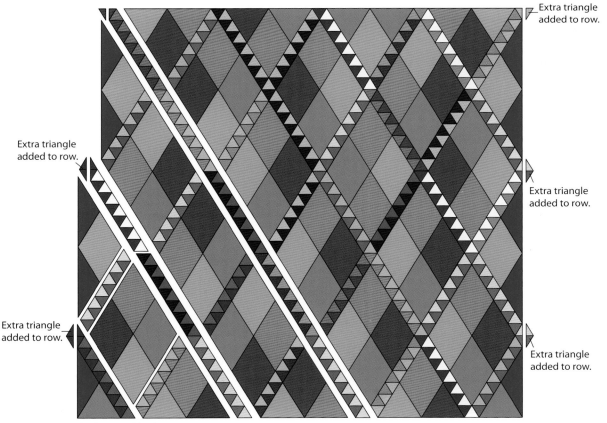

Extra triangle added to row.

Extra triangle added to row.

Extra triangle added to row.

Extra triangle added to row.

Extra triangle added to row.

Quilt assembly diagram

The quilting lines in this quilt connect the 60° lines between the diamonds and triangles.

How I Finished

Batting that does not have scrim is preferred for hand quilting. Scrim is a process that makes batting stronger if it is going to be machine quilted. Without scrim, it needles beautifully, and generally the final product is as light as a feather. To quilt, I used a variety of matching perle cottons size 8. I like to start with three to five colors that work with the fabrics in the quilt. The added colors and textures are just another beautiful layer of interest when the quilt is finished. The lines are spaced about 2″ apart in a diagonal grid pattern, which supports the 60° angle of the design as well as adding a nice layer of texture to the quilt.

Big Fluffy Love

FINISHED QUILT: 88½″ × 98″ (225cm × 249cm)

How I Started

Big Fluffy Love is the result of two design forces coming together. First, fabric designers are giving us lovely soft flannels in colorful combinations that are great fun to use. Second, hexagons are a mad craze, so it was only a matter of time before someone would make them big and with flannel! This quilt is made with Anna Maria Horner's designs, which are gorgeous flowers in a variety of sizes. Flowers are pretty, but it is important to use graphic prints like plaids, stripes, and spots to create a sense of movement throughout the quilt. The flower center and border fabrics are one of the simpler designs and create a bit of space in the quilt. The use of a large hexagon template makes cutting the hexagons fun and easy. They can be fussy cut to feature parts of the design or not—whatever you prefer. I like random, but in some cases I got a bit of extra fabric to fussy cut a particular element of the design. In this case, I surrounded the inner hexagon with flower fabrics.

To complement the softness of the flannel I used voile for the backing fabric, which has several advantages. It is wide, so for large quilts two lengths of fabric are adequate. More importantly it has a soft, silky texture that shows up the quilting beautifully in a wide range of beautiful patterns and designs. This one will be on my bed in the cold winter months!

MATERIALS

Yardage based on 42″ (107cm) usable WOF.*

11 FLANNELS:

- ½–1 yard (45–90cm) of each flannel, totaling at least 7½ yards (6.5m) for flower petals (Note that ¾ yard will yield 2 whole sets of flower petals. Fussy cutting requires more yardage, depending on pattern repeat.)

2 ADDITIONAL FLANNELS:

- 1¾ yards (1.6m) for flower centers
- 2 yards (2m) for border

BACKING: 5½ yards (5.1m), 54″ (137cm) wide

BINDING: ⅞ yard (80cm)

BATTING: 97″ × 106″ (250cm × 270cm)

OPTIONAL TOOL:

- Hexagon template with 5″ finished sides
- Alternatively, use template plastic to make template from pattern (pullout page P2).

* WOF = width of fabric

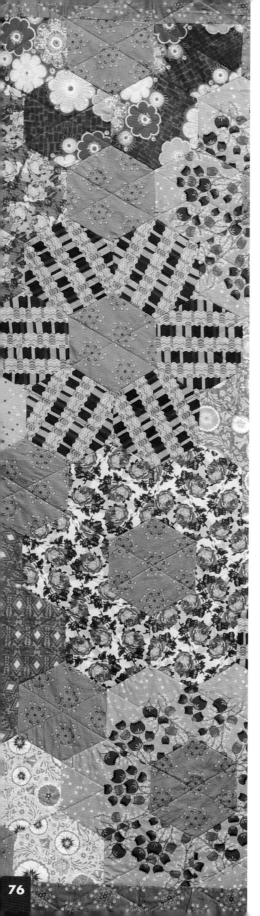

CUTTING

From flannels:

- Measure the height of your template across 2 parallel sides. Cut all the flannel fabrics, except the border fabric, into strips that height × WOF, and then cut hexagons across the strips. You should be able to cut 4 hexagons from each strip of fabric, and 3 WOF strips will yield enough hexagons for 2 whole sets of flower petals.

- Place the template as shown, with 2 sides aligned with the raw edges of the strip and the points to each side. Cut on the right side against the template; then slide a ruler to the left of the template and remove the template to cut the left side. Repeat to cut a total of 114 hexagons (24 for the flower centers and 90 for the petals).

Cut strip of fabric 9″ × WOF and use template to subcut hexagon shapes along length.

From border fabric:

- Cut 10 strips 6½″ × WOF.

From binding fabric:

- Cut 10 strips 2½″ × WOF.

Construction

All seam allowances are ¼" unless otherwise noted.

1. Sew a matching flower hexagon to each side of a blue center hexagon, sewing from point to point only and not into the seam allowances, and backstitching at the beginning and end of each seam. If you are using a directional print or fussy-cut hexagon, make sure to place each hexagon correctly.

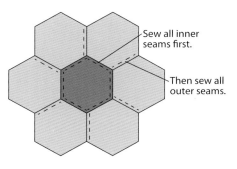

Sew from point to point only.

2. When all 6 hexagons are attached to the center, sew the inset connecting seams, starting from the center hexagon and finishing at the outer edge of the flower, again backstitching at the beginning and end of each seam.

Sew all inner seams first.

Then sew all outer seams.

note

To be very accurate, mark the junction of the ¼" seam allowances at each corner of the hexagon on the reverse side and sew only to this point. If you are confident in measuring these points by eye while you are sewing, then don't worry about marking. Reverse or take a few stitches in place on your sewing machine to secure the seams at each end where marked.

3. Repeat Steps 1 and 2 to make 10 whole flowers. Then make up the following partial flowers:

A. *5-petal flower:* Make 2.

B. *4-petal flower:* Make 4.

C. *3-petal flower, without a center:* Make 1.

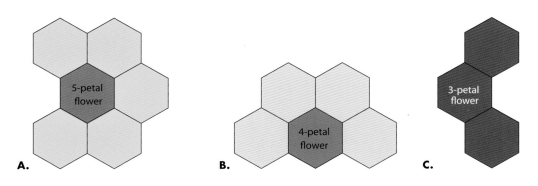

5-petal flower

4-petal flower

3-petal flower

A.

B.

C.

Assembly

1. Place the whole flowers and partial flowers on your design wall, using the quilt assembly diagram as a guide. Fill in the empty spaces with additional blue center hexagons and a single petal.

2. Sew the sections of the quilt together, first joining the individual hexagons to the adjacent flowers.

3. Join the flowers in rows *or* columns by starting at an outer edge, aligning the raw edges, and backstitching at the beginning of the seam. Stitch to the corner, stop with the needle down, and pivot, shifting the next 2 hexagons so that the raw edges are aligned. Stitch to the next corner and repeat until you have sewn 2 flowers together, backstitching at the end of this seam.

4. Continue to sew all the sections together, constantly returning pieces to your design wall and checking that all the pieces are in the right places.

5. When the quilt top is complete, trim back the flowers along the edges with a ruler and rotary cutter to make a straight edge around the quilt.

6. Join the 6½″ × WOF border strips end to end into a continuous strip.

7. Refer to Butted Borders (page 34) to measure the quilt top and cut and attach the borders.

8. Layer, baste, and quilt. Join the 10 binding strips end to end with diagonal seams and use them to bind the quilt.

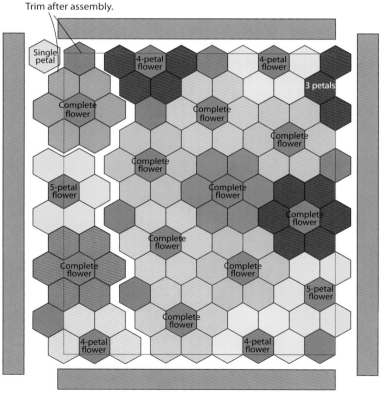

Quilt assembly diagram

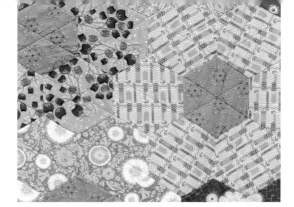

How I Finished

Big Fluffy Love was machine quilted in diagonal lines on a 60° angle, dissecting each hexagon. Alternatively, you could quilt with perle cotton, either in lines or outlining each hexagon.

Snuggle up! You'll feel the love!

Dream Catcher

9 FINISHED BLOCKS: 24″ × 24″ each • **FINISHED QUILT:** 88″ × 88″ (224cm × 224cm)

How I Started

I am a huge fan of stripes! I love them and use them all the time to add immediate graphic energy to my quilts. In this case, I saw an antique quilt made in the 1920s that was string pieced. I loved the layout of the blocks and thought, "Hmm, no time for sewing all those strips together, so how about these great stripes?" This quilt came together really easily using three different color-ways of Kaffe Fassett's Marquee Stripe fabric combined with solid fabrics.

The setting quarter-square triangle blocks are made easy as well with the use of the Creative Grids 90° strip ruler. I love a good tool, especially when multiples of triangles need to be cut and sewn. Cutting them accurately at speed means I'll finish the job before I get bored. If the bold version doesn't do it for you, try using a soft-color or muted stripe.

MATERIALS

Yardage based on 42″ (107cm) usable WOF.*

STRIPED FABRICS: 1⅔ yards (1.4m) each Marquee Stripe in pastel, bright, and husky (or 3 different related stripes) for blocks

OTHER FABRICS: 1⅛ yards (1m) red solid and a total of 3½ yards (3.2m) of assorted solid colors (or 50 assorted strips 2½″ × WOF) for quarter-square triangle units

BACKING: 8¼ yards (7.6m)

BINDING: ¾ yard (70cm)

BATTING: 96″ × 96″ (245cm × 245cm)

OPTIONAL TOOL:

• 90° Strip Ruler for Quarter-Square Triangles (by Creative Grids)

• Alternatively, use template plastic to make templates from patterns (pullout page P3).

* WOF = width of fabric

CUTTING

From each striped fabric:

If the stripes run lengthwise (parallel to the selvages), cut 4 strips *on the lengthwise grain* 8½″ × length of fabric. If the stripes run on the crosswise grain, cut 6 strips 8½″ × WOF. Crosswise-striped fabric must have at least a 42″ usable width, or you will need additional fabric.

1. Use the 45° line on your rectangular ruler to cut at a 45° angle across an 8½″-wide strip as shown.

2. Measure 25¼″ along the bottom of the strip to mark the base of the triangle and then cut another 45° angle as shown to make the shape.

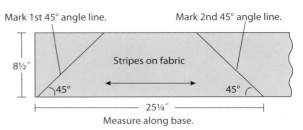

Mark 1st 45° angle line.   Mark 2nd 45° angle line.

8½″   Stripes on fabric

45°   45°

25¼″
Measure along base.

3. Measure 25¼″ along the top of the strip and make another 45°-angle cut to make a second shape.

4. Repeat Steps 1–3 to cut a total of 36 shapes.

From solid fabrics:

• Refer to Using Special Rulers: Quarter-Square Triangle Units (page 17), to cut 16 red and 50 other solid color strips 2½″ × WOF using the Creative Grids 90° Strip Ruler for Quarter-Square Triangles. Then, using the ruler or the pattern (pullout page P3), subcut the strips into 784 triangles.

Binding:

• Cut 9 strips 2½″ × WOF.

Sewing

All seam allowances are ¼" unless otherwise noted.

BLOCKS

1. Select 4 of the large stripe shapes. Lay them out so that the blunt ends form an empty square in the center. Then fill the empty square with 4 sets of 4 single solid triangles, arranged to make 4 quarter-square

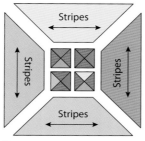

Do *not* sew any pieces together yet.

triangle (QST) units. Place a pair of red triangles opposite each other in each QST unit, oriented as shown so that the inner red triangles make a pinwheel, and randomly alternate the other colors. Do *not* sew the pieces together yet.

2. Separate the arranged solid triangles so that 4 form the point of a large triangle with the striped shape as the base.

3. Join a red and a different solid triangle along the long edges to form the center of the pieced triangle tip. Sew the remaining triangles to either side of this unit. By doing this, you avoid inset seams when sewing the entire block together later.

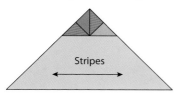

Sew triangles together in above formation for easy construction.

4. Sew the long edge of the pieced triangle tip from Step 3 to the blunt edge of the striped shape to create a pieced triangle.

5. Repeat Steps 3 and 4 to make a total of 4 pieced triangles.

6. Lay out the 4 completed triangles back into a square shape. Sew in pairs and then sew the pairs together to complete the block.

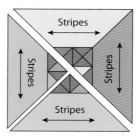

7. Repeat Steps 1–6 to make a total of 9 blocks.

SASHING STRIPS

1. From the remaining red and solid triangles, sew 2 different solid triangles together along the short sides. Repeat to make an identical pair. Sew the pairs together along the long sides to make a QST unit.

2. Repeat Step 1 to make a total of 160 QST units. Set aside 16 QST units to use as cornerstones.

3. Sew 6 QST units together to form a sashing strip. Repeat this step to make a total of 24 sashing strips.

Assembly

1. Refer to the quilt assembly diagram to lay out the 9 completed blocks in 3 rows of 3. Join them into rows with sashing strips between the blocks, beginning and ending with a sashing strip.

2. Sew 4 cornerstones and 3 sashing strips together to make a sashing row, beginning and ending with a cornerstone.

3. Repeat Step 2 to make a total of 4 sashing rows.

4. Pin to match the joins and sew the block rows and sashing rows together.

5. Layer, baste, and quilt. Join the 9 binding strips end to end with diagonal seams and use them to bind the quilt.

Quilt assembly diagram

How I Finished

Dream Catcher was custom machine quilted by
Adri van der Zel. We examined the lines of the
block and selected lines that created a secondary
pattern. The quilting adds texture without
interfering with the design of the quilt.

Big Wedding

FINISHED QUILT: 88" × 88" (224cm × 224cm)

How I Started

All wedge rulers make pieces that join to form a circle. When I realized one day that the Wedding Ring block is made with intersecting circles, it was a short leap to take one of my favorite patterns and one of my favorite tools and get them working together. The "Read All About It!!" newspaper-print linen serves as a great neutral background fabric. The blades are made with fabric from a new Australian designer, Veritas Designs by Verity Hinwood. The palette is simple, and only a few fabrics were used to make a strong statement.

MATERIALS

*Yardage based on 42" (107cm) usable WOF.**

BACKGROUND: 5 yards (4.6m), 55" (140cm) wide

CORNERSTONES AND EYES:
- ⅞ yard (80cm) of dark gray fabric for cornerstones only
- 1¼ yards (1.2m) of black fabric for cornerstones and center eyes

BLADES:
- ⅞ yard (80cm) gray floral fabric
- ⅞ yard (80cm) taupe floral fabric
- ⅞ yard (80cm) white text fabric
- ⅞ yard (80cm) green fabric

BACKING: 8¼ yards (7.5m)

BINDING: ¾ yard (70cm)

BATTING: 96" × 96" (245cm × 245cm)

TOOLS: I used a 13½"-long 10° wedge ruler, measuring 2¼" at the narrow end and 4¾" at the wide end (or use pattern, pullout page P1).

* WOF = width of fabric

CUTTING

Cornerstones:

- Cut 4 squares 13½″ × 13½″ from each of the 2 cornerstone fabrics.

- Cut 4 of the center eye shapes from the black fabric using the pattern (pullout page P1), adding your preferred seam allowance for needle-turn appliqué.

Blades:

- Cut 2 strips 13½″ × WOF from each of the 4 blade fabrics.

  Refer to Cutting Wedges from Strips (page 15) to cut a total of 72 blades from the strips cut in Step 1, using a 10° wedge ruler or the pattern provided (pullout page P1) to make your own template. Each strip will provide approximately 12 blades. If you are using a ruler that is taller than your strip of fabric, mark the ruler so that the wide end is 4¾″ and the narrow end is 2¼″.

Background:

Note: If you want to match the pattern, you may need extra yardage.

- Cut the background fabric into 2 equal lengths and trim off the selvages. Find the center of each length, pin along the length with right sides together, and sew.

Binding:

- Cut 9 strips 2½″ × WOF.

tip

Cutting wedges is made easy by marking the cutting measurements with masking tape. Use them as a guide to place the wedge ruler correctly each time.

Construction

All seam allowances are ¼" unless otherwise noted.

1. Arrange the blades into 8 groups of 9 blades, with an equal distribution of the colors. Vary the color placement in each group. Sew the blades together as shown to make 8 sets of pieced units.

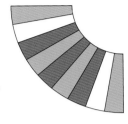

2. Lay out 2 pieced units with a matching 13½" × 13½" cornerstone square at each end as shown. Sew a square to each end of a pieced unit; then

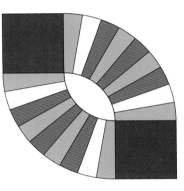

match the points, pin, and join the 2 squares to the other pieced unit to form a complete eye shape. Repeat this step to make a total of 4 pieced eye shapes.

3. Position a center eye shape in the middle of the pieced eye from Step 2. Match the ends of the eye piece to the inner corners of the squares and secure in place with pins. Needle-turn appliqué the eye to the pieced unit. Repeat this step with all 4 pieced eye units.

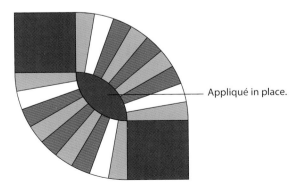

Appliqué in place.

Assembly

1. Lay out the 4 units to form a large ring as shown in the quilt assembly diagram, alternating the color placement of the cornerstones.

2. Pin 2 eyes together at the cornerstones and sew together. Repeat to join all 4 pieced eyes into 1 unit that is open at the center.

3. Fold the background in half vertically and horizontally and press the folds to mark the quarters of the background.

4. Place the pieced ring on the background, aligning the seams joining the cornerstones with the folds on the background. Be sure the rings are as flat as possible. Baste in place.

tip

I recommend basting the ring with thread instead of glue. Thread basting is quick and allows for adjustments as you move around the ring, to make the placement accurate.

5. Appliqué the ring to the background. Trim the background to the desired finished size *plus 1″*.

6. Layer, baste, and quilt. Join the 9 binding strips end to end with diagonal seams and use them to bind the quilt.

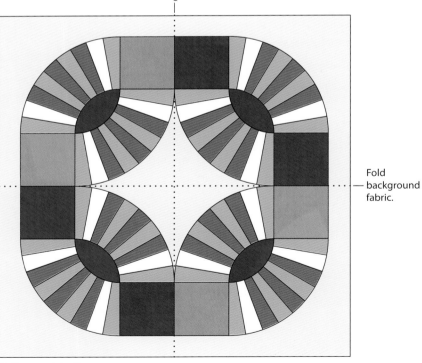

Fold background fabric.

Fold background fabric.

Quilt assembly diagram

How I Finished

Adri van der Zel quilted *Big Wedding*. We always talk about what we like in the fabrics and design of the quilt before discussing design options for quilting. In this case the background is quilted in a wonky crisscross pattern that resembles the Nets prints by Brandon Mably used in the big squares. Adri and I agree that minimalist quilting is a great way to go with contemporary-style quilts. It is always satisfying to work with a quilter who understands where I am going with my quilts.

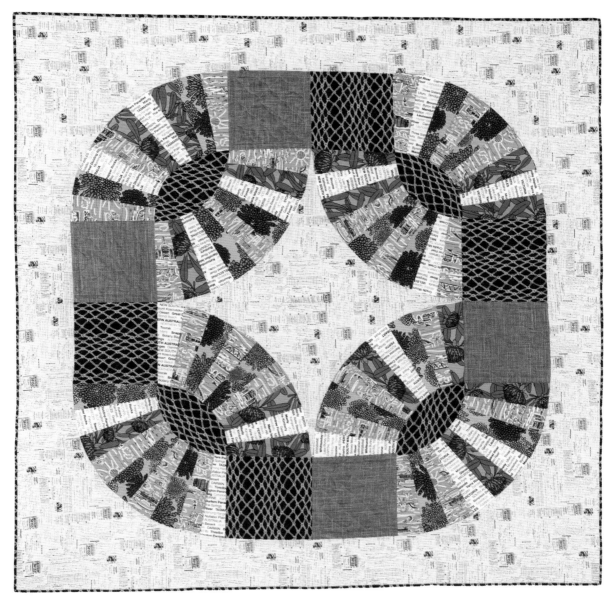

Adding Layers—Color, Design & Imagination

CHAPTER 3
Working with Scale

One of the things I tend to avoid when selecting a quilt pattern is small, fiddly block construction. First, these blocks take ages, and second, I like to use large graphic floral prints. As a result, my mind took me on a path of exploring the idea of scale. What happens if we make a block *big ... really big*? The fabric really shows and the quilt is relatively easy! Problems solved! Then I started playing with the concept of the pattern moving beyond the barrier of the quilt edge. This really got my imagination engaged. What happens if we mix big and small together? The puzzle in this process was how to maintain the feeling of tradition while exploring the blown-out size structure. In some cases I just couldn't resist the large scale to show off the fabrics, but in others an element of design requires time and concentration, which maintains the integrity of tradition.

Basket Case

FINISHED QUILT: 92" × 92" (234cm × 234cm)

How I Started

I was leafing through an antique quilt book when I stopped to stare at a basket quilt. In typical traditional style for this pattern, there were a lot of little baskets. Although I loved the look of them all in a row, the thought of making so many tiny baskets seemed a bit, well, tedious. *Bing!* I suddenly saw it big and realized that by using the simple half-square triangle block I could make the whole quilt in a jiffy. It started coming together a bit too easily, so I also pieced the background with little squares, just for fun!

The basket fabrics are from Kaffe Fassett. I had two large pieces of fabric of the same pattern in two colors in my stash. As the quilt grew, I gathered other stash fabrics that had similar colors and value for the extra baskets. The background fabrics are a collection of pretty light-colored selections that I had on hand. Piecing them together gave me the effect of a patterned background.

note

Selecting fabrics that have a similar effect across a quilt is one of my favorite skills to practice. The fabrics need to feel the same but have a slight point of difference that makes them interesting.

MATERIALS

Yardage based on 42" (107cm) usable WOF.*

Baskets:

FABRIC 1: 1¾ yards (1.6m) orange print for main basket, handle, and sashing

FABRIC 2: ¾ yard (70cm) dark orange print for top basket and sashing

FABRIC 3: ¾ yard (70cm) brown print for side basket and sashing

FABRIC 4: ⅝ yard (60cm) plum print for corner basket and sashing

FABRIC 5: 2½ yards (2.3m) purple print for baskets and sashing

Background:

2¾ yards (2.5m) total of light-value warm colors (pink, yellow, light orange, light red, gold) or 36 strips 2½" × WOF plus a few scraps at least 4" × 4"

2¾ yards (2.5m) of light-value cool colors (lavender, light green, light blue) fabrics or 36 strips 2½" × WOF plus a few scraps at least 4" × 4"

Backing:

8⅝ yards (7.9m)

Binding:

¾ yard (70cm) of stripe fabric

Batting:

100" × 100" (255m × 255m)

* WOF = width of fabric

Basket Case

CUTTING

Fabric 1:

1. To draw the basket handle, fold a 22½" × WOF strip in half, wrong sides together. Measure up along the fold and make a mark at 17½" and another 3" past the first mark. Repeat measuring and marking the same distances from the fold along the base of the fabric.

2. Use a string compass (a length of string attached to a pencil point) to draw an arc from outer point to outer point, drawing the arc with your dominant hand and holding the string at the corner of the folded fabric with the other hand. Repeat to connect the inside marks. Cut out the handle piece through both layers, adding a ³⁄₁₆" needle-turn seam allowance beyond the drawn lines. Finger-press the fabric to the wrong side along the drawn lines. Set aside the remaining fabric for the sashing.

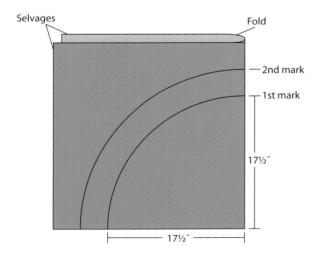

3. Cut 2 strips 12⅞" × WOF and subcut 4 squares 12⅞" × 12⅞". Cut the squares in half on the diagonal once to make 8 half-square triangles for the basket blocks.

4. Cut the remaining fabric from the handle plus 1 additional strip into 4⅞" × WOF strips for the sashing triangles.

Fabrics 2 and 3 (from each):

1. Cut 1 strip 12⅞" × WOF and subcut 3 squares 12⅞" × 12⅞". Cut the squares in half on the diagonal once to make 5 half-square triangles for the basket blocks.

2. Cut 2 strips 4⅞" × WOF for the sashing triangles.

Fabric 4:

1. Cut 1 strip 12⅞" × WOF and subcut 2 squares 12⅞" × 12⅞". Cut the squares in half on the diagonal once to make 3 half-square triangles for the basket blocks.

2. Cut 1 strip 4⅞" × WOF for the sashing triangles.

Fabric 5:

1. Cut 4 strips 12⅞" × WOF and subcut 10 squares 12⅞" × 12⅞". Cut the squares in half on the diagonal once to make 19 half-square triangles for the basket blocks.

2. Cut 6 strips 4⅞" × WOF for the sashing triangles.

Binding:

Cut 10 strips 2½" × WOF.

Preparation

All seam allowances are ¼" unless otherwise noted.

BACKGROUND

To achieve this scrappy-looking background, work your stash and grab colors from a variety of piles as long as they are light. Choose some that are warm in hue and some that are cool. Alternating the warm and cool combinations keeps the colors from pooling in groups. Push yourself to make interesting combinations of light fabrics that work together to form a unified background with highs and lows.

1. Cut the background fabrics into 72 warm and 72 cool strips 2½" × 21". This makes it easier to use scraps for this project, and it makes for more variety in your finished background blocks.

2. Make 2 piles: warm colors and cool colors. Sew the strips together along the length in pairs of 1 warm and 1 cool strip.

tip

To avoid issues with bias when sewing strips together, trim them to equal lengths before sewing them together. Match the centers of the strips and pin along the length. Reverse the direction of sewing as you join sets—which means sewing alternating seams up or down.

3. Sew 3 pairs of strips into a set of 6 strips and press all the seams in the same direction.

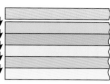

4. Fold the strip set so the long edges are aligned, right sides together, and then sew into a tube.

Sew into a tube along the length.

5. Flatten the tube on your cutting mat and carefully cut across the tube to make loop strips that are 2½" wide. Unpick the seams of these tubes at different points along the way so that the strips start with different colors.

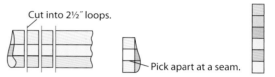

Cut into 2½" loops.

Pick apart at a seam.

Cut tube into 2½"-wide loops and pick seam apart at varying points in each loop.

6. Repeat Steps 3–5 until you have 132 strips with 6 squares each.

7. Sew 6 different loop strips together to make a background block. Orient the strips so seam allowances will nest. Repeat this step to make a total of 22 background blocks.

Make 22 background blocks.

8. Cut an additional 3 strips 4″ × WOF from the background fabrics. Subcut the strips into a total of 21 squares 4″ × 4″. Subcut each square on the diagonal twice to make 84 quarter-square triangles.

9. Use the remaining loop strips from Step 7 and unpick seams at varying points to yield 14 strips each of 1, 2, 3, 4, and 5 squares. Join a quarter-square triangle to the end of each strip, making sure that the triangle's long edge is facing the same direction on each strip, as shown below.

10. Lay out the strips in descending order. Match the joins, pin, and sew together to make 14 pieced background half-square triangles.

BASKETS

1. Sew a large Fabric 5 half-square triangle to a different large half-square triangle along the long edges in the following quantities:

- 6 with Fabric 1
- 3 each with Fabrics 2 and 3
- 1 with Fabric 4

2. Sew pieced background triangles to the remaining large half-square triangles along the long edges in the following quantities:

- 2 each of Fabrics 1, 2, 3, and 4
- 6 of Fabric 5

SASHING STRIPS

The sashing is made of half-square triangle (HST) units sewn with 1 small triangle of Fabric 5 and 1 small triangle from another basket print. *Be sure to match the orientation of the fabrics in the pieced baskets as you assemble the sashing strips.*

1. Pair each purple 4⅞″ × WOF strip with a strip of one of the other 4 basket fabrics, right sides together, and subcut into 4⅞″ × 4⅞″ squares. Subcut the paired squares once on the diagonal to make 90 half-square triangles for the sashing.

2. Sew a pair of triangles from Step 1 together along the long edge. Be careful not to tug or stretch the bias edge out of shape. Repeat this step to make a total of 88 HST units.

3. Join the HST units in rows in the following combinations, making sure to orient all the Fabric 5 triangles in the same direction:

- Make 2 sashing strips with 23 HST units.
- Make 2 sashing strips with 15 HST units.
- Make 2 sashing strips with 6 HST units.

Assembly

1. Follow the quilt assembly diagram to sew the basket blocks and pieced background squares together in partial rows, between the vertical sashing strips, as shown.

2. Sew the partial rows together as shown.

3. Position the basket handle as shown and then pin, baste, and needle-turn appliqué in place. Unpick the diagonal seams on the basket blocks at the ends of the handle, slip the handle inside, and then machine sew the seams closed again.

4. Sew a 15-unit sashing strip to the bottom of the left-hand section of Row 2, making sure the Fabric 5 triangles are oriented in the same direction in both. Be sure to match all the points in the long seams.

5. Sew a 6-unit sashing strip to the bottom of the right-hand section of Row 2.

6. Repeat Steps 3 and 4 to sew the same size sashing strips to the bottom of Row 7.

7. Sew the left-hand row sections together.

8. Sew the right-hand row sections together.

9. Sew 23-unit sashing strips to the left sides of both the left-hand and right-hand sections of the quilt.

10. Sew the 2 sections together to complete the quilt top.

11. Layer, baste, and quilt. Join the 10 binding strips end to end with diagonal seams and use them to bind the quilt.

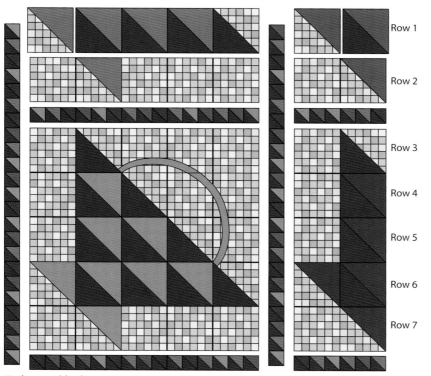

Quilt assembly diagram

Layering Your Quilt

Lay out the backing fabric right side down (having joined the fabric where required) on a flat surface. If you are laying it out on the floor, secure it with masking tape around the edges, taking care not to pull the fabric too tight. Place the batting over the backing fabric and smooth it out from the center to the outer edges. Lay the quilt top right side up over the batting. Smooth the quilt top out from the middle to the edges. Baste or pin through all three layers. This is also known as a quilt sandwich.

How to Make a Hanging Sleeve

You can use scrap fabric to make a hanging sleeve to thread a curtain rod through, enabling you to hang the quilt on a wall. Make the hanging sleeve when you are attaching the binding. This is a tedious job to remember when finishing a quilt, but it is worthwhile if you are planning to hang your quilt. Building the sleeve into the quilt during construction ensures that it is done properly.

1. Measure your quilt across the top. Cut a 7″-wide strip of fabric that is about 4″ shorter than this measurement. (Piece if needed.)

2. Fold and press the short ends of the strip in ¼″ to the wrong side twice and sew to hem the ends. Fold and press the strip in half lengthwise, wrong sides together, align the raw edges with the top edge of the unbound quilt, and pin the sleeve in place.

3. From the binding fabric, cut the required number of 2½″ × WOF strips to fit end to end around the outside of the quilt. Sew the strips together end to end at a 45° angle. (Doing this eases the bulk of the seam along the edge of the quilt and avoids big lumpy joins.) Trim the excess fabric from the joining seams and press the strip in half, wrong sides together, along its entire length.

4. Align the raw edges of the binding strip with the raw edges of the quilt. Leaving about 3″ at the start, sew the binding in place, mitering the corners as you go. Stop sewing a few inches before reaching your starting point. Fold ½″ at the beginning end of the binding into itself, and then tuck the end of the binding strip into the folded section. Make sure the binding lies flat and then finish sewing it to the quilt.

5. The sleeve is machine sewn to the back of the quilt when attaching the binding.

6. Now get comfortable, flip the binding over to the back of the quilt, and slipstitch it into place all the way around the quilt.

7. After you have finished slipstitching the binding down, fold and press the top layer of the sleeve up even with the outside edge of the binding and then back down the back of the quilt.

8. Slipstitch the lower edge of the sleeve to the back of the quilt, leaving the sleeve gaping enough to fit a curtain rod through it.

That's it. You're done. Congratulations!

How I Finished

One of my favorite quilting patterns is to simply quilt diagonal lines. It has great rhythm in the process and often suits a quilt with a nice traditional slant. For *Basket Case*, I hand quilted using a variety of light-colored perle cottons size 8. I drew the initial lines with a chalk pencil and ruler on the diagonal, but once I had the line in my eye, I freehand quilted through each square.

Lily Field

FINISHED QUILT: 84″ × 102″ (213cm × 259cm)

How I Started

When a new line of Kaffe Fassett fabrics arrives, it is nearly impossible not to take immediate action with the rotary cutter due to the visually exciting nature of the fabrics. *Lily Field* started just that way. I grabbed the fabrics I couldn't resist first: several new redder-than-reds by Kaffe, a gorgeous green rose by Phillip Jacob, and a field of daisies on lavender and a dynamic plaid by Brandon Mably. These designers give us dependable fabric lines a few times a year, and although the designs might change, the colors are consistently available. I rarely use only six fabrics, but in this case it suited the task for the baskets, flowers, and background perfectly.

The Carolina Lily is a favorite block, and soon it started to take shape. It is a beautiful block made with half-square triangles. I started with the three *big* blocks on the design wall. From there it took a series of layout changes to arrive at a design that I am now happy with. The funny part of this is that it just kept growing. Each sewing session indicated that I needed more and more and more of the 6″ × 6″ blocks. I loved the rhythm of the half-square triangle sewing. I made heaps, sewed them into rows, and sewed the rows into flowers. Then I tried other sizes. Then made more! Keeping the block simple meant that I could experiment with the scale of the blocks over and over again. In the end I decided on three sizes.

MATERIALS

Yardage based on 42″ (107cm) usable WOF.*

REDS: 3⅞ yards (3.5m) total of 3–5 fabrics of similar value

GREEN FLORAL: 2¾ yards (2.5m)

LAVENDER: 4½ yards (4.1m) for background

PLAID: 1 yard (90cm) for center medallion border

BACKING: 8 yards (7.3m)

BINDING: ⅞ yard (80cm)

BATTING: 92″ × 110″ (235m × 280m)

OPTIONAL TOOL: 45° Strip Ruler for Half-Square Triangles (by Creative Grids)

* WOF = width of fabric

CUTTING

From green floral:

Flowerpot base:
- Cut a strip 14⅝" × WOF. Subcut 1 square 14⅝" × 14⅝", and then cut in half once on the diagonal to yield 2 half-square triangles.
- From the remaining strip, cut 1 square 14¼" × 14¼" and 2 squares 6⅛" × 6⅛". Subcut the smaller squares in half on the diagonal twice for 8 quarter-squares for the flowerpot rim.

3 large lilies:
- Cut a strip 8⅞" × WOF. Cut 3 squares 8⅞" × 8⅞". Subcut on the diagonal once for 6 half-square triangles.
- Cut 1 strip 8½" × WOF. Subcut 3 squares 8½" × 8½".

14 medium lilies:
- Cut 2 strips 4⅞" × WOF. Subcut 14 squares 4⅞" × 4⅞"; subcut again on the diagonal once for 28 half-square triangles.
- Cut 1 strip 4½" × WOF. Subcut 14 squares 4½" × 4½".

50 small lilies:
- Cut 4 strips 2⅞" × WOF. Subcut 50 squares; subcut again on the diagonal once for 100 half-square triangles.
- Cut 4 strips 2½" × WOF. Subcut 50 squares 2½" × 2½".

Setting squares:
- Cut 3 strips 6½" × WOF. Subcut 16 squares 6½" × 6½".

Stems:
- Cut 1 strip 2½" × WOF. Subcut into 1 piece 2½" × 25½" for the long stem and 2 pieces 2½" × 5" for the short stems.

From reds:

3 large lilies:
- Cut 3 strips 8⅞" × WOF. Subcut 12 squares 8⅞" × 8⅞"; subcut again on the diagonal once for 24 half-square triangles.

14 medium lilies:
- Cut 7 strips 4⅞" × WOF. Subcut 56 squares 4⅞" × 4⅞"; subcut again on the diagonal once for 112 half-square triangles.

50 small lilies:
- Cut 15 strips 2⅞" × WOF. Subcut 200 squares 2⅞" × 2⅞"; subcut again on the diagonal once for 400 half-square triangles.

From lavender:

3 large lilies:
- Cut 2 strips 8⅞" × WOF. Subcut 6 squares 8⅞" × 8⅞"; subcut again on the diagonal once for 12 half-square triangles.
- Cut 1 strip 8½" × WOF. Subcut 3 squares 8½" × 8½".

14 medium lilies:
- Cut 4 strips 4⅞" × WOF. Subcut 28 squares 4⅞" × 4⅞"; subcut again on the diagonal once for 56 half-square triangles.
- Cut 2 strips 4½" × WOF. Subcut 14 squares 4½" × 4½".

50 small lilies:

- Cut 8 strips 2⅞" × WOF. Subcut 100 squares 2⅞" × 2⅞"; subcut again on the diagonal once for 200 half-square triangles.

- Cut 4 strips 2½" × WOF. Subcut 50 squares 2½" × 2½".

Medallion:

Flower Pot block:

- Cut 1 square 17⅞" × 17⅞". Subcut on the diagonal once for 2 half-square triangles.

- Cut 2 squares 6⅛" × 6⅛". Subcut on the diagonal twice to make 8 quarter-square triangles for the pot rim (1 will be extra).

Medallion sashing:

- Cut 2 strips 4" × 24½" for the medallion sashing.

Corner units:

- Cut 1 strip 6½" × WOF. Subcut 4 squares 6½" × 6½" for the bottom 2 corner units.

- Cut 2 strips 9¾" × WOF. Subcut 7 squares 9¾" × 9¾"; subcut again on the diagonal twice to make 28 quarter-square setting triangles for the corner sections.

From plaid:

- Cut 7 strips 4½" × WOF for the medallion border.

From binding:

- Cut 10 strips 2½" × WOF.

Sewing

All seam allowances are ¼" unless otherwise noted.

Group the cut pieces so that you have the following configurations of half-square triangle units and squares, and sew as directed. The construction for each Lily block is a basic nine-patch, regardless of the size. Arrange the 9 squares in the correct layout, match and pin through the points, and then sew to make nice neat lilies.

LILY BLOCK CONSTRUCTION

1. Make half-square triangle units in the following quantities:

FINISHED SIZE	LARGE 8" × 8"	MEDIUM 4" × 4"	SMALL 2" × 2"
Lavender/red	12	56	200
Green/red	6	28	100
Red/red	3	14	50

Press and trim all the dog-ears.

2. Arrange the half-square triangles, 1 lavender background square, and 1 green square of the same size in 3 rows of 3 as shown. Sew the half-square triangle (HST) units and squares into rows.

3. Sew the rows together to complete the block.

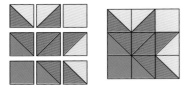

Lily block assembly

Repeat Steps 1–3 to make the following blocks with the appropriately sized squares and triangles:

LARGE LILY BLOCK (24" × 24" FINISHED): Make 3 blocks using the green and lavender 8½" × 8½" squares and large half-square triangle units.

MEDIUM LILY BLOCK (12" × 12" FINISHED): Make 14 blocks using the green and lavender 4½" × 4½" squares and the medium half-square triangle units.

SMALL LILY BLOCK (6" × 6" FINISHED): Make 50 blocks using the green and lavender 2½" × 2½" squares and the small half-square triangle units.

Assembly

FLOWER POT BLOCK

1. Join the 2 green 14⅝″ half-square triangles to 2 adjacent sides of the green 14¼″ × 14¼″ square to form a larger triangle.

2. Make the top of the pot rim by joining 7 lavender quarter-square triangles to the 8 green quarter-square triangles along the short sides in a row; start and end with a green triangle.

3. Join the pieced triangle strip to the green pot base on the long side as shown, pinning to match the center and points at the ends.

4. Sew the 2 lavender 17⅞″ half-square triangles together along the short sides to make a large triangle. Handle carefully, as the outer edge of this block will be on the bias.

5. Sew the long side of the pieced lavender triangle to the top of the pot rim.

6. Prepare the green stems for appliqué by finger-pressing to the back along the length of the stems so that the sides meet at the center on the wrong side. The finished stem should be about 1¼″ wide. Glue or pin the stem into place over the center seam of the pieced lavender triangle. There will be extra at either end of the stem, but do *not* trim it yet.

Flower Pot block
assembly

7. Do the same for the 2 short stems, positioning one end under the long stem and leaving extra at the other end, which will be tucked into the seams when the medallion is assembled.

Stem appliqué
placement

8. Open up the sewn seams where the long stem meets the pieced pot rim and insert the end of the stem into the seam at the top of the pot. Then appliqué all the stems in place along their length. Sew the pot rim seams closed again.

CENTER MEDALLION

1. Lay out the 3 large Lily blocks and the Flower Pot block as shown, and ensure that the flowers are facing the correct directions.

2. Sew 2 Lily blocks together as shown with a 4″ × 24½″ sashing strip between them.

3. Sew a 4″ × 24½″ sashing strip to the top of the bottom right Lily block.

4. Sew the Flower Pot block and the sashed Lily block together, tucking the loose ends of the stems into the seam allowance before stitching.

5. Sew the top and bottom rows together to complete the center medallion, again tucking the loose ends of the stems into the seam allowance before stitching.

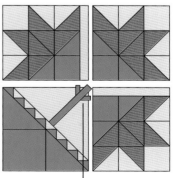

Tuck stem ends
between blocks before
joining blocks.

Center medallion assembly

MEDALLION BORDER

1. Join the 7 plaid 4½″ × WOF strips end to end into a continuous strip and then cut 4 border strips 4½″ × 65½″.

2. Refer to Mitered Corner Borders (page 33) to attach the borders to the center medallion.

CORNER SECTIONS

1. Start with the top left corner and lay out 6 medium Lily blocks, 4 green 6½″ × 6½″ squares, 14 small Lily blocks, and 7 lavender setting triangles as shown. Sew the units together in columns as shown.

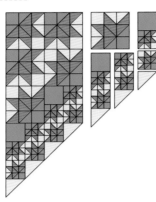

Top corner section

2. Sew the columns together.

3. Repeat Steps 1 and 2 to make a reversed corner section for the top right corner.

4. The bottom corner sections are different from the top corner sections. Lay out 1 medium Lily block, 2 lavender 6½″ × 6½″ squares, 4 green 6½″ × 6½″ squares, 11 small Lily blocks, and 7 lavender setting triangles as shown. Sew together in columns as shown.

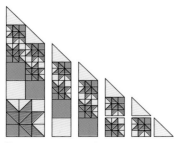

Bottom corner section

5. Sew the columns together.

6. Repeat Steps 4 and 5 to make a reversed corner section for the bottom right corner.

QUILT TOP

1. Sew the bottom corner sections to the bottom of the center medallion.

2. Match the points and pin the long sides of the top corner sections to the top of the center medallion. Sew just to the pins—do not sew into the seam allowances.

3. Sew the vertical seam between the 2 top corner sections to complete the quilt top.

4. Layer, baste, and quilt. Join the 10 binding strips end to end with diagonal seams and use them to bind the quilt.

Quilt assembly diagram

How I Finished

This quilt was professionally quilted by Adri van der Zel, with whom I have a well-established relationship. I start a conversation based on how I see the quilt lines. She then applies her expert viewpoint and gets to work. In the end it is an effective collaboration combining both the effect of the fabric and the pattern into lines that draw attention to both. To make sure you get what you want, it is important to talk through your vision with the machine quilter before handing the project over.

Mega Churn Dash

FINISHED QUILT: 91″ × 91″ (231cm × 231cm)

How I Started

We see a lot of pretty quilts made of beautiful flowers in pinks and other soft colors, but what do we do for the men in our lives? The *big* pattern and strong lines of this quilt present a great opportunity to make a masculine quilt for your special guy. Easy to make, yes, but not lacking in visual interest.

The fabrics are by David Butler from his Curious Nature line; they are home decorator weight but don't need to be. I just liked the contrast and thought it would be handy to make a nice, heavy quilt for my son Noah to use in the colder winter months. Australia is generally thought of as a warm climate, but when it does get cold with no central heating, we get cold!

MATERIALS

For 56″-wide (140cm) fabrics:

FEATURE FABRIC: 3⅓ yards (3m)

BACKGROUND FABRIC: 2⅛ yards (2m)

BACKING: 5⅝ yards (5.2m)

BINDING: ⅝ yard (60cm)

BATTING: 99″ × 99″ (255cm × 255cm)

For 42″-wide (107cm) fabrics:

FEATURE FABRIC: 4 yards (3.7m)

BACKGROUND FABRIC: 2¾ yards (2.5m)

BACKING: 8½ yards (7.8m)

BINDING: ⅞ yard (80cm)

BATTING: 99″ × 99″ (255cm × 255cm)

tip

Any high-contrast fabric in gray, brown, navy, or even green would make this a handsome project.

This is a simple quilt to make using contrasting fabrics with a dramatic effect. In this version I used 2 strong contrasting fabrics and made it even more dramatic by making the block into the center of a bigger Churn Dash block, and then that finished block into the center of an even *bigger* Churn Dash block—Mega Churn Dash!

CUTTING

note

The instructions are written so that the largest pieces of the blocks are cut first. This rule should *always* be followed, unless specifically instructed otherwise. Use the cutting diagrams (next page) for the most efficient way to cut the pieces. If your fabric is 56″ (140cm) wide or wider, you will be able to cut 2 large squares from 1 WOF* strip. If not, you will have room for only 1 large square but will be able to use the remaining strip to cut large rectangles.

WOF = width of fabric

Churn Dash blocks:

From feature fabric:

- **Large blocks:** Cut 2 squares 27⅞″ × 27⅞″ and 4 rectangles 14″ × 27½″.

- **Medium blocks:** Cut 2 squares 9⅞″ × 9⅞″ and 4 rectangles 5″ × 9½″.

- **Small blocks:** Cut 2 squares 3⅞″ × 3⅞″ and 4 rectangles 2″ × 3½″.

- **Border:** Cut 7 strips 5½″ × WOF (8 strips if using narrower fabric). Cut 2 squares 5⅞″ × 5⅞″ for the border corners.

From each square above, subcut through the diagonal once to make 4 half-square triangles of each size.

From background fabric:

- **Large blocks:** Cut 2 squares 27⅞″ × 27⅞″ and 4 rectangles 14″ × 27½″.

- **Medium blocks:** Cut 2 squares 9⅞″ × 9⅞″ and 4 rectangles 5″ × 9½″.

- **Small blocks:** Cut 2 squares 3⅞″ × 3⅞″ and 4 rectangles 2″ × 3½″. Also cut 1 square 3½″ × 3½″ for the center.

- **Border:** Cut 2 squares 5⅞″ × 5⅞″ for the border corners.

From each square above (except the 3½″ × 3½″ square), subcut through the diagonal once to make 4 half-square triangles of each size.

Binding:

- If using fabric 56″ (140cm) wide or wider, cut 8 strips 2½″ × WOF. If using fabric that is only 42″ (107cm) wide, cut 10 strips 2½″ × WOF.

Adding Layers—Color, Design & Imagination

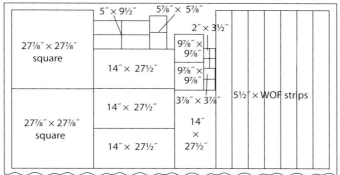

Fabric 56″ (140 cm) wide or wider

- 27⅞″ × 27⅞″ square
- 27⅞″ × 27⅞″ square
- 5″ × 9½″
- 5⅞″ × 5⅞″
- 14″ × 27½″
- 14″ × 27½″
- 14″ × 27½″
- 2″ × 3½″
- 9⅞″ × 9⅞″
- 9⅞″ × 9⅞″
- 3⅞″ × 3⅞″
- 14″ × 27½″
- 5½″ × WOF strips

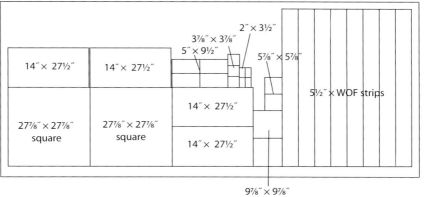

Fabric less than 56″ (140cm) wide

- 14″ × 27½″
- 14″ × 27½″
- 27⅞″ × 27⅞″ square
- 27⅞″ × 27⅞″ square
- 5″ × 9½″
- 3⅞″ × 3⅞″
- 2″ × 3½″
- 5⅞″ × 5⅞″
- 14″ × 27½″
- 14″ × 27½″
- 5½″ × WOF strips
- 9⅞″ × 9⅞″

Cutting diagrams

Construction

All seam allowances are ¼″ unless otherwise noted.
Half-Square Triangle Units

Pin a feature fabric half-square triangle (HST) and a background fabric HST, both the same size, right sides together along the diagonal (bias) edges. Sew the pair together along the pinned edge carefully. Note: This seam is on the bias and therefore will be stretchy and easily pushed or pulled out of shape. Press the seam allowances toward the darker fabric.

Repeat to sew all pairs of all sizes of HSTs together. Set aside the 4 HST units sewn from 5⅞″ triangles for the border corners.

Half-square triangle unit

TWO-RECTANGLE SQUARES

Sew a feature fabric rectangle and a background fabric rectangle, both the same size, right sides together along the *long* edges. Press the seam allowances toward the darker fabric.

Repeat to sew all pairs of all sizes of rectangles together.

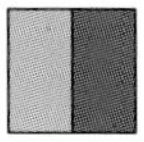

Two-rectangle square

Assembly

CHURN DASHES

1. Start with the small Churn Dash. Lay out the units in 3 rows of 3 using the photo (page 115) or quilt assembly diagram (below) as your guide. The top and bottom rows are made up of 2 of the small HST units and 1 small two-rectangle square. The middle row is made up of 2 small two-rectangle units and the 3½″ × 3½″ background fabric square. Double-check that you have oriented all the units so that the Churn Dash pattern is clear to see.

2. Sew the 3 units of each row together and press lightly.

3. Sew the 3 rows together, taking care to pin the seam joins to form neat points between the squares. Press lightly again to finish.

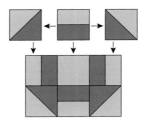

This is the small Churn Dash, which will be the central square of the medium Churn Dash block.

4. Repeat Steps 1–3, using the small Churn Dash as the central square in the middle row and the medium HST units and medium two-rectangle squares.

This is the medium Churn Dash, which will be the central square of the large Churn Dash block.

5. Repeat Steps 1–3, using the medium Churn Dash as the central square in the middle row, and the large HST units and large two-rectangle squares.

BORDER

1. Sew the 5½″ × WOF strips together end to end to make a continuous strip.

2. Measure the quilt through its center from top to bottom and from side to side. It should measure 81½″ × 81½″.

3. Cut the border strip into 4 pieces 5½″ × 81½″ each (or the measured length and width of your quilt's sides).

4. Pin a border strip to each side of the quilt, first pinning the 2 ends and then along the length. Sew and then press the seams toward the borders.

5. Refer to the quilt assembly diagram to sew the border corner HST units set aside earlier to each end of the remaining 2 border strips as shown, making sure the units are oriented correctly to give the impression that the border has rounded corners. Press the seams toward the border.

6. Pin the remaining strips to the top and bottom of the quilt, again checking the orientation of the corner squares. Pin both ends first, then along the length of each border. Sew in place. Press the seams toward the borders.

7. Layer, baste, and quilt. If you want to add a hanging sleeve (page 100), do it now. Join all the binding strips end to end with diagonal seams and use them to bind the quilt.

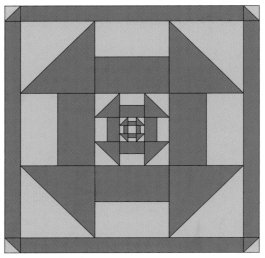

Quilt assembly diagram

How I Finished

I handed the quilt over to Adri van der Zel, who custom quilted it by machine. With this one we liked the oval graphic in the print and chose that quilting design for a lot of the open areas. This quilt is made with home decorator fabric so it is already heavy. We thought a minimum of quilting would suit the style and materials used. I put a hanging sleeve on all my quilts, as they often spend a long time hanging in the shop. See How to Make a Hanging Sleeve (page 100) to prepare your own quilts for hanging before you attach the binding.

Super Nova

FINISHED QUILT: *72" × 84" (183cm × 214cm)*

How I Started

I love working with big stars. The math is easy to scale up and down while keeping the shape recognizable. The real stars in this quilt are some of my favorite fabric designers. The large shapes allow the fabulous detail and color of the fabrics to be on full display. Anna Maria Horner is a big player in my stash. I love her use of imagination, which takes me to a special place of grandma hugs and childhood whispers. Melissa White, a decorative artist from England, brings style from the ancient halls of English castles and the designs of yesterday to play at patchwork in an updated palette. And no colorful display of contemporary fabric artists would be complete without Amy Butler. Her use of timeless graphics in new colors has changed the landscape of design.

So, how do you decide where the fabrics will be placed? Quantity has a lot to do with it. If I love a fabric, I buy a lot of it, and when the urge strikes to use it, it becomes a big player. Next, select fabrics that create the same amount of impact, for example, equal-value similar-sized beautiful flowers. If a star overpowers the others, it has to go. Conversely, if the star disappears in comparison to the others, either add more of it or exchange it for a stronger fabric. Pay attention to what your eyes tell you and act accordingly!

The background black-and-white fabric is my favorite neutral for sustaining colorful fabrics. This one has a lot of energy, so it might not be for the fainthearted. I like to push the boundaries a bit and see what happens. You could use a spot or any evenly spaced regular pattern. You won't be able to match patterns, so be wary of plaids or stripes. What is really fun with this pattern is how the stars that run off the quilt take your mind with them to outer space!

MATERIALS

*Yardage based on 42" (107cm) usable WOF.**

FABRIC 1: 1⅛ yards (1m) large floral for largest star

FABRIC 2: ¾ yard (70cm) brown floral for large star points

FABRIC 3: ⅜ yard (35cm) lime green print for large star points

FABRIC 4: ⅓ yard (30cm) light blue small-scale print for small stars

FABRIC 5: ½ yard (50cm) pink floral for medium corner star

FABRIC 6: ½ yard (50cm) multicolored floral for medium corner star

FABRIC 7: ½ yard (50cm) maroon floral for medium corner star

FABRIC 8: 3¼ yards (3m) for background

BACKING: 5¼ yards (4.8m)

BINDING: ¾ yard (70cm)

BATTING: 80" × 92" (205cm × 235cm)

* WOF = width of fabric

CUTTING

Always cut the larger pieces first and the smaller pieces last.

Fabric 1:

- Cut 1 square 24½″ × 24½″ for the center of the largest star.

- Cut 3 squares 12⅞″ × 12⅞″ and subcut each on the diagonal once to make 6 half-square triangles for the points of the largest star.

Fabric 2:

- Cut 4 squares 12⅞″ × 12⅞″ and subcut each on the diagonal once to make 8 half-square triangles for the large star points.

Fabric 3:

- Cut 2 squares 12⅞″ × 12⅞″ and subcut each on the diagonal once to make 4 half-square triangles for the large star points.

Fabric 4:

- Fussy cut 3 squares 6½″ × 6½″ for the centers of the small stars.

- Cut 12 squares 3⅞″ × 3⅞″ and subcut each on the diagonal once to make 24 half-square triangles for the small star points.

Fabrics 5, 6, and 7 (from each fabric):

- Cut 1 square 16½″ × 16½″ for the center of a medium corner star.

- Cut 2 squares 8⅞″ × 8⅞″ and subcut each on the diagonal once to make half-square triangles for the points of a medium corner star.

Fabric 8:

- Cut 3 squares 25¼″ × 25¼″ and subcut on the diagonal twice to make 12 quarter-square triangles for the backgrounds of all the large star points. (You will have 3 extra.)

- Cut 2 squares 17¼″ × 17¼″ and subcut on the diagonal twice to make 8 quarter-square triangles for the backgrounds of the medium corner star points. (You will have 2 extra.)

- Cut 5 squares 12½″ × 12½″ for the large star block corners and large background squares.

- Cut 3 squares 8½″ × 8½″ for the medium star block corners.

- Cut 3 squares 7¼″ × 7¼″ and subcut on the diagonal twice to make 12 quarter-square triangles for the backgrounds of the small star block points.

- Cut 1 strip 3½″ × WOF* and subcut into 12 squares 3½″ × 3½″ for the small star block corners.

Binding:

- Cut 9 strips 2½″ × WOF for the binding.

Construction

All seam allowances are ¼″ unless otherwise noted.

SMALL STAR BLOCKS

1. Sew a 3⅞″ half-square triangle along the long (bias) edge to each short (bias) edge of a 7¼″ background fabric quarter-square triangle as shown. Press.

2. Repeat Step 1 to make a total of 4 small star point units.

3. Sew a star point unit from Step 1 to each side of a fussy-cut 3½″ × 3½″ square as shown to make the center row of the star block. Press.

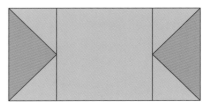

4. Sew a 3½″ × 3½″ background square to each end of a star point unit as shown to make the top row. Press. Repeat this step to make the bottom row.

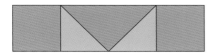

5. Sew the 3 rows together as shown to make the star block. Press.

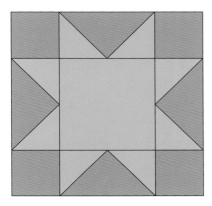

6. Repeat Steps 1–5 to make a total of 3 small star blocks.

MEDIUM CORNER STAR BLOCKS

1. Refer to Small Star Blocks, Step 1, to make a star point unit with 2 matching floral 8⅞″ half-square triangles and 1 background 17¼″ quarter-square triangle. Repeat to make a second matching star point unit.

2. Sew a medium star point unit to one side of a matching 16½″ × 16½″ square.

3. Referring to the quilt assembly diagram (page 120) for the orientation of the units, sew a background 8½″ × 8½″ square to a medium star point unit.

4. Again referring to the quilt assembly diagram for orientation, sew the rows created in Steps 2 and 3 together to make a medium corner star block.

5. Repeat Steps 1–4 to make a total of 3 medium corner star blocks.

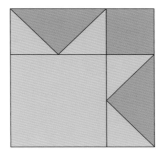

LARGE STAR BLOCK / LARGE STAR POINTS

1. Refer to Small Star Blocks, Step 1, to make a star point unit with 2 matching floral 12⅞″ half-square triangles and 1 background 25¼″ quarter-square triangle. Repeat this step with all the remaining triangles of this size to make a total of 9 large star point units.

2. Referring to the quilt assembly diagram for orientation, repeat Steps 2 and 3, Medium Corner Star Blocks, to make the center row and a top and bottom row, using the floral 24½″ × 24½″ square, 3 matching floral star point units from Step 1, and 2 background 12½″ × 12½″ squares.

3. Again referring to the quilt assembly diagram for orientation, sew the rows created in Step 2 together to make the large star block.

Assembly

1. Use your design wall to arrange the completed stars and star points to your liking, or follow the quilt assembly diagram.

2. Refer to the quilt assembly diagram to sew the star blocks and background squares together in quadrants as shown, first sewing the units into short rows and then into quadrants, and pressing after each seam.

3. Sew the 2 left-hand quadrants into a column. Sew the 2 right-hand quadrants into a column. Sew the columns together.

4. Layer, baste, and quilt. Join the 9 binding strips end to end with diagonal seams and use them to bind the quilt.

Quilt assembly diagram

And voilà!

How I Finished

Adri van der Zel machine quilted *Super Nova* by following the diagonal lines of the points and mirroring the seamlines anywhere from one to three times, with the quilting lines set about ½″ apart.

As in all the large-scale quilts, the machine quilting follows the lines of the quilt. The stars echo in and out but allow for space between the lines.

Star Man

FINISHED QUILT: 80″ × 90″ (203cm × 229cm)

How I Started

Here we have a dynamic quilt with bold use of a simple pattern structure that is sure to appeal to that young man; it might even stay with him from his cuddly kid days until he is master of his domain! *Star Man* is easily constructed with a series of half-square triangles, a few big quarter-squares, and ... well ... squares! It is flannel so it has snuggle appeal. You know him; he loves the soft touch but is too tough to admit it. The stars are easily made in any color grouping you like. These flannels are from the Maywood Studio Woolies Flannel collection and include a lot of print choices—such as spots, herringbone, plaids, and tweeds—as well as soft solids. Each year the company produces a line of great basic colors, so this quilt is one I am sure you can make today!

note

Working with luscious, thick flannels is easier when the blocks are big. The quilting lines stabilize the quilt but keep it simple.

tip

Using light-, medium-, and dark-value fabrics in 3–5 color groups will make each star just a bit different. If you have the right amount of fabrics you can arrange the blocks any way you like to create more obvious stars—or less obvious stars! The stronger the contrast in value, the more you will see the stars. The colors given are for the quilt as shown, but you can use any colors you want as long as you have enough on hand.

MATERIALS

Yardage based on 42″ (107cm) usable WOF.*

FLANNELS: 9 yards (8.3m) total of a variety of dark-, medium-, and light-value flannels in gray, blue, white, cream, yellow, orange, red, and brown. You will need a minimum of 10⅝″ × WOF of each fabric chosen.

BACKING: 5⅝ yards (5.2m) fabric (requires minimum 44″ [112cm] usable fabric width, or additional yardage to piece)

BINDING: ¾ yard (70cm)

BATTING: 88″ × 98″ (225cm × 250cm)

* WOF = width of fabric

CUTTING

Cut the big shapes first. Use the photo (page 126) as a diagram for color.

Here are 3 ways to create a reliable side setting triangle, a necessity for these shapes.

- **Option 1:** Cut strips 10⅝″ × WOF. Establish a 45° angle, using the line on your rotary cutting ruler, and cut along this line. Measure 21¼″ along the base of the strip. Cut the second 45° angle as shown to meet the top point.

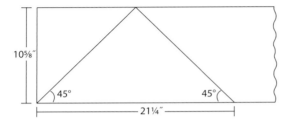

- **Option 2:** Cut a 21¼″ × 21¼″ square on the diagonal twice to make 4 quarter-square triangles (QSTs).

- **Option 3:** If you want to use large scraps for more variety, like my quilt, use the pattern (pullout page P4), making sure to place the long side of the triangle on the straight grain of the fabric.

Large triangles:

- Using one of the options (at left), cut 18 large quarter-square triangles for the background of the star points. All but 3 of my large triangles were cut from light values to make the stars pop out.

Small half-square triangles:

- Cut at least 18 medium- and dark-value 10⅞″ × 10⅞″ squares. Cut each square in half diagonally once to yield 2 half-square triangles (HSTs). You need a total of 36 HSTs for the star points. If you want more variety, cut more squares and use only 1 of the 2 HSTs, or use the half-square triangle pattern (pullout page P3) to cut from large scraps.

Squares:

- Cut a total of 36 squares 10½″ × 10½″. (I used 14 light squares and 22 medium and dark squares in my quilt.)

Binding:

- Cut 9 strips 2½″ × WOF for the binding.

Assembly

All seam allowances are ¼″ unless otherwise noted.

1. Group the squares and small and large triangles in any color combinations you like.

2. Join 2 smaller HSTs, along their long sides, to the bias (short) sides of a QST to make a Flying Geese unit. Repeat this step to make a total of 18 Flying Geese units.

3. Follow the quilt assembly diagram and lay out the Flying Geese units and 10½″ × 10½″ squares to make stars.

4. Sew the 10½″ × 10½″ squares into pairs horizontally to make 18 total two-patch units.

5. Sew the Flying Geese units and two-patch units together into rows. For Rows 3 and 6, first sew 2 sets of two-patch units together to make a four-patch and then sew the four-patch to a Flying Geese unit, making sure to pin to match the star points and the four-patch seams.

6. Pin to match the points and sew the rows together.

7. Layer, baste, and quilt. Join the 9 binding strips end to end with diagonal seams and use them to bind the quilt.

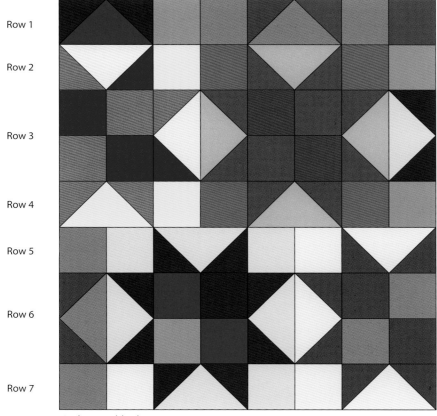

Row 1
Row 2
Row 3
Row 4
Row 5
Row 6
Row 7

Quilt assembly diagram

How I Finished

Grace Widders quilted *Star Man* on a domestic machine. We discussed the design and decided that quilting lines parallel to the seams but 1″ on either side would reinforce the shapes used in the quilt and add linear interest.

About the Author

resources

MATERIAL OBSESSION
materialobsession.com.au
Fabrics, templates, and kits

CREATIVE GRIDS
creativegridsusa.com
Rulers and templates

C&T PUBLISHING
ctpub.com
*Quilter's Freezer
Paper Sheets*

Kathy says she often looks back on her youth and thinks of the simplicity of green grass yards in Ohio. Cowboys and Indians, hide-and-seek, cards, and coloring filled her days. She liked nothing more than climbing a tree, taking aimless walks in the woods, or going for long bike rides. Sewing was not on her list of favorite activities! She moved several times—from Ohio to New York and back again—before heading off to college in the foothills of the Appalachian Mountains, where she was surrounded by more wilderness. Upon graduating she left the wild for a different kind of wild—the East Village of New York City during the punk rock era. She worked in advertising, fashion, and marketing for ten years. While living in the city she was often grateful for the foundation of green grass of her youth, she says. Then, she married and moved with her husband to Australia in 1990, where she was able to give her sons the foundation of green grass and a simple, practical life. Her three nearly adult sons are fully Aussie, having grown up playing cricket and rugby.

In 1993 she made her first quilt and instantly fell in love with the "American"-style quilt. It connected her to her childhood and her home so far away and simple pleasures. She spent years making squares until she discovered triangles. Then she found an array of lively shapes and skills that took her into more complex quilting patterns. She enjoys that there is a lot to learn in quilting, and she says she will always want to fine-tune and add skills to the basics that she still loves. She connects with the idea of traditional quilts made modern by the influences of today. She says the many artists with whom she has worked over the years have opened her eyes to the principles of design, color, shape, and line; they include Sue Cody, Marg George, Brigitte Giblin, Wendy Williams, Rosalie Dace, and so many others. Now she wishes to share the added depth she has found as she has grown in her love.

In 2003 she opened Material Obsession and found the companionship needed to make life complete, people who share this patchwork passion with her! The shop is a place where quilters are encouraged to experiment with textiles, design, and method. It is a creative environment that is all about the discovery of adding layers one at a time. She hopes to extend that environment via this book.

You can find out more about her life, family, and shop at the Material Obsession blog: materialobsession.typepad.com.

stashBOOKS®

fabric arts for a handmade lifestyle

If you're craving beautiful authenticity in a time of mass-production...Stash Books is for you. Stash Books is a line of how-to books celebrating fabric arts for a handmade lifestyle. Backed by C&T Publishing's solid reputation for quality, Stash Books will inspire you with contemporary designs, clear and simple instructions, and engaging photography.

www.stashbooks.com